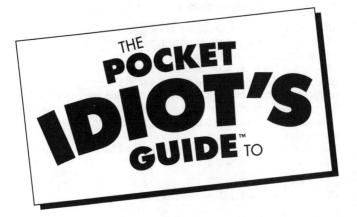

THE

POCKET
IDIOT'S
GUIDE™ TO

Choosing &
Training a Dog

by Sarah Hodgson

alpha
books

A Division of Macmillan General Reference
A Simon & Schuster Macmillan Company
1633 Broadway, 7th Floor, New York, NY 10019-6785

©1997 Sarah Hodgson

International Standard Book Number: 0-87605-281-2
Library of Congress Catalog Card Number: 97-20855

99 98 97   8 7 6 5 4 3 2

Interpretation of the printing code: the rightmost number of the first series of numbers is the year of the book's printing; the rightmost number of the second series of numbers is the number of the book's printing. For example, a printing code of 97-1 shows that the first printing occurred in 1997.

Printed in the United States of America

Editorial Manager: Gretchen Henderson
Editors: Beth Adelman, Richard A. Thomas, Jr.
Production/Copy Editor: Lynn Northrup
Cover Designer: Michael Freeland
Cartoonist: Judd Winick
Designer: Glenn Larsen
Indexer: Nadia Ibrahim
Production Team: Angela Calvert, Kim Cofer, Linda Knose

Contents

Introduction

Right off the bat, I just want to say that you're not an idiot. At least I don't think so. You may feel like one, but that's due to a lack of appropriate information rather than stupidity. And that's the whole focus of this book: good information to guide you.

Just so you know, I love dogs. Actually, "love them" is, perhaps, an understatement. I have this habit of sitting down on the ground whenever I see a dog to whisper lovingly into its ears and shower it with kisses. Yes, I even do this with dogs I've never met before—after I check to make sure they're safe, of course.

To me, there is nothing more appealing than a healthy, well-mannered dog. They're fun to have and to be around. They're the ultimate in stress reduction. On the other hand, an unhealthy, untrained dog is a sorry sight. Why own a dog if you're not going to train it and take care of it?

Now, I know most of you reading this book probably have an untrained dog, but there is a difference between you and the vast majority of people with untrained dogs: You're admitting your shortcomings and doing something about them. Asking for help (by buying and reading this book) is the first step in solving the problem.

So let's not waste time. Whether you're starting off with a puppy or an older dog, this book covers it all. You can read it cover to cover, but you really don't have to. For example, the first few chapters talk about choosing and buying a dog. If you've already done that, why read them? You might start off with a lot of regrets, and I don't want you to do that. No matter how many mistakes you've made so far, you probably haven't scarred your dog for life, so why be hard on yourself? The best way to approach this *read-a-book-and-train-a-dog* project is to read through the Table of Contents or flip around the Index and find the best place to jump in.

What I Do All Day

I do have a real job, in addition to writing this book for you. I am a dog teacher—or perhaps I should say I'm a people teacher. I'm absolutely crazy about my work.

Some days, I help people decide what breed to buy or to select a good family dog from a litter of pups. Every day is different. In addition to providing private help, I also teach group classes—Puppy Kindergarten, Grade School, High School, and College—which is a whole different experience. The mix is quite exciting.

Needless to say, I get a lot of experience coping with a wide array of dogs and an even wider array of people, the culmination of which is this book and its two predecessors: *The Complete Idiot's Guide to Choosing, Training, and Raising a Dog* and *The Complete Idiot's Guide to Fun and Tricks With Your Dog.*

In this book, I'm going to try to account for every lifestyle, dog personality, and problem that could arise in your day-to-day life. Together, we'll explore all sorts of "What should I do?" scenarios and "What if that doesn't work?" alternatives. Because every dog is different, many instructions will be presented for different dog personalities. And because you, dear readers, have different schedules and life commitments, I'll try to address those, too.

The Extras

One of the perks in reading (and writing) this book is the little boxes that are sprinkled throughout the text. They're added to draw your attention to important information or facts that will make it easier for you to train your dog.

Sarah Says

The Sarah Says tips simplify each process and clue you in to shortcuts. These tips may also highlight how to handle dogs with different temperaments.

Doglish

Doglish boxes define key terms you'll need to know to get up to speed in the dog world.

Grrr

Don't forget to read the Grrr warning boxes! These will caution you about common errors and dangerous handling habits, such as holding the collar too tightly.

Chapter 1

A Breed-by-Breed Analysis

TELL ME ABOUT YOUR LITTER...

In This Chapter

➤ How breeding got started with domestication

➤ Breeds and the American Kennel Club (AKC)

➤ Breed characteristics and mixed breeds

If you're thinking about adding a dog to your family, it's important that you consider a suitable breed. Know what you and your family want and know what the breed was bred to do. The rest of this chapter describes the seven breed groups assigned by the American Kennel Club (AKC) and lists the breeds that fall into each breed group. These descriptions, along with Chapter 2, "Lifestyle and Litters," will help you find a breed to go with your personality and start off with a dog who can live up to your expectations!

The 142 breeds registered with the AKC are subdivided into seven groups: Sporting, Hound, Working, Herding, Non-Sporting, Terrier, and Toy. Each group shares common

characteristics. To add another spin on this breed search, I
have broken the groups into subgroups and listed which
breeds fall under each description. Confused? Feeling
dizzy? Read on; it's quite simple. The following table ex-
plains what I mean when I refer to various sizes of dogs.

Sarah Says

Please note that I refer only to the breeds
recognized by the AKC. There are roughly
400 breeds recognized worldwide.

Dog Size Chart

Category	Height	Weight
Small	Up to 5 inches	2–13 pounds
Medium	6–15 inches	14–45 pounds
Large	16–24 inches	46–90 pounds
Giant	25+ inches	91+ pounds

The Sporting Group

The dogs in this group were bred to aid man in hunting
fowl (wild birds). Conditioned by nature to retrieve, these
dogs can be trained to gather birds from the field or water
or can simply stay at home and make excellent companions fetching tennis balls, slippers, and the morning paper. There are four types of dogs in the Sporting group:
pointers, retrievers, spaniels, and setters.

The Pointers

Tall, leggy dogs, bred to spend entire days running the
fields looking for land fowl, these dogs are competitive,

attentive, and *very* energetic. Without sufficient exercise, the pointing breeds have an abundance of nervous energy, which may result in destructive chewing, digging, jumping, and excessive barking. Given lots of exercise, however, you'll find them friendly, involved, and accepting of children. The pointers love an active lifestyle!

German Shorthaired
Pointer

German Wirehaired
Pointer

Pointer

Vizsla

Weimaraner

Wirehaired Pointing
Griffon

German Shorthaired Pointer

The Retrievers

Also in the Sporting group, retrievers were bred to stay close to their masters and retrieve water fowl (or nets, in the case of the Portuguese version!). Well-built, large dogs, they're a bright, loyal, and active lot. Happy souls, they love to be involved in all family activities, take to training very well, and generally view all strangers as potential friends. Easy-going, retrievers make excellent family pets, but prolonged isolation upsets them. They may develop

Hyper Isolation Anxiety, resulting in destructive chewing, digging, barking, and jumping.

Chesapeake Bay Retriever   Golden Retriever

Curly-Coated Retriever   Labrador Retriever

Flat-Coated Retriever

Labrador Retriever

The Spaniels

The low-riders of the Sporting group, spaniels were bred to find and flush birds. Trusting and friendly, spaniels fit in well with active families. Loyal, spaniels love family excursions and children, but don't like being left alone. If isolated or untrained, spaniels may become timid, whine a lot, or guard their food and other objects. As with all breeds, buy spaniels from experienced breeders only.

Clumber Spaniel   Irish Water Spaniel

Cocker Spaniel   Sussex Spaniel

English Cocker Spaniel   Water Spaniel

English Springer Spaniel   Welsh Springer Spaniel

Field Spaniel

English Springer Spaniel

The Setters

Majestic setters, bred to run the fields and point and flush fowl, are also part of the Sporting group. Highly intelligent, they are loyal, non-protective dogs who thrive on family interaction. As a bonus, you'll look terrifically aristocratic as you stroll through town with a setter at the end of a leash. Exercise is a requirement for these large fellows; without it, they get high-strung and nervous.

Brittany	Gordon Setter
English Setter	Irish Setter

Irish Setter

The Hound Group

You ain't nothing but a hound dog. (Sorry, I just had to get that in.) These breeds like following fast-moving game, and this penchant has won them over to the hunting circles. In addition to their keen noses or sharp eyesight, their easy-going and, at times, stoic personality has endeared them as family pets. There are three types of hounds: Sight, Scent, and Large Game hounds.

The Sighthounds

Relying on their eyesight to course fast-moving game, these sighthound breeds have been domesticated to make placid, gentle pets. The instinct to run after fast-moving targets, however, has never been bred out of the sighthounds—they'll need to be leashed when outdoors because you won't outrun them! In addition, they need to be socialized with common household critters at an early age so they won't confuse them with lunch. Sighthounds are alert and mild and make wonderful pets in stable households.

Afghan Hound	Irish Wolfhound
Basenji	Pharaoh Hound
Borzoi	Saluki
Greyhound	Scottish Deerhound
Ibizan Hound	Whippet

Greyhound

The Scent Hounds

Bred to follow scent, these hound breeds are active, lively, and rugged. That sensitive nose, however, makes them somewhat difficult to train; they'd rather trail a rabbit than hang around learning to Sit and Stay. A leash or enclosure is required when these dogs are outside—that nose again! Although a bit stubborn when it comes to training, scent hounds are happy breeds. Sweet, lively, and tolerant, they thrive on family involvement and accept children and strangers with ease.

American Foxhound	Dachshund
Basset Hound	English Foxhound
Beagle	Harrier
Black and Tan Coonhound	Otterhound
Bloodhound	Petit Basset Griffon Vendéen

Basset Hound

The Large Game Hounds

As you might guess, these hounds are large, powerful, and fearless when challenged, as they were originally bred to hunt lions and elk. No longer used for their original purpose, the large game hounds now enjoy life as pets and watchdogs. All are strong-willed and independent and need training to enhance their sociability—and your control. These dogs are steady and calm and make devoted pets in the right home. But don't expect them to back down from an argument! Exercise and socialize these dogs to prevent destructive habits or territorial aggression.

Norwegian Elkhound

Rhodesian Ridgeback

Rhodesian Ridgeback

The Working Group

This classification needs little explanation. Though more varied in job description than the other groups, these breeds have one thing in common—throughout the centuries they have had a specific job to do and humans have been the beneficiaries. The subgroups are Sled/Draft, Estate Guarding, Personal Protection, and Rescue.

The Sled/Draft Dogs

These working dogs, also referred to as Nordic breeds, love cold weather! Originally bred to pull sleds and live outside, sled dogs have thick, beautiful coats and a strong instinct to pull. Put one on the end of a leash and you'll see what I mean! Rugged and free-spirited, sled dogs need plenty of exercise and thrive outdoors. Don't try to coddle these dogs—they're not the cushion-by-the-fire type! Although strong-willed and hard to train, Nordic breeds make sweet, friendly pets if you work with them. They need exercise and attention to prevent destructive behavior. These fearless hunters will wander if given the opportunity.

Sledding:	Draft:
Alaskan Malamute	Bernese Mountain Dog
Samoyed	Greater Swiss Mountain Dog
Siberian Husky	

Grrr

With their double coat, sledding breeds aren't much for really hot weather. If you live in a hot climate, consider another breed. These dogs would be miserable.

Siberian Husky

The Guard Dogs

Bred to protect territories and livestock without man's direction, the guard breeds are alert, intelligent, courageous, and independent. These dogs need structured training and a qualified leader. Please be sure you are up to the job—you must be the shepherd, not the sheep. Guard dogs living in a sheep's home may attack strangers who enter their territory. But in the right home (with the right owner), these dogs are calm, dignified, and devoted. Train and socialize them early to avoid later difficulties.

Akita	Komondor
Bullmastiff	Kuvasz
Great Dane	Mastiff
Great Pyrenees	Rottweiler

Great Pyrenees

The Personal Protection Dogs

These dogs were bred to work under the direction of man. Consequently, they are intelligent, strong-willed, and intensely loyal to one family unit. These dogs need a structured training program and early socialization to offset potential territorial aggression. For the determined and committed owner, these dogs make extraordinary companions. Without training and exercise, however, they may become aggressive, unruly, and destructive.

Boxer	Giant Schnauzer
Doberman Pinscher	Standard Schnauzer

Doberman Pinscher

The Rescue/Water Dogs

The rescue breeds are large, low-key dogs with dense coats. They prefer cold weather to hot. Steady and intelligent, rescue breeds are exceptional around children when raised with them. Untrained and isolated, however, they can develop Hyper Isolation Anxiety.

> Newfoundland
>
> Portuguese Water Dog
>
> Saint Bernard

Saint Bernard

The Herding Group

The function of these breeds is as it sounds: to herd live-stock. They're a hard-working crowd of dogs who, in most cases, work under the direction of a shepherd. This group can be broken down into two types: sheep herders and cattle herders.

The Sheep Herders

These herding dogs were not bred to guard the flock, but to move it. They are agile, alert, and very active. Easily trained, the sheep herders are devoted to their family, not prone to roaming, and tolerant of children. They can be protective of their property and suspicious of strangers, but they are not generally prone to serious aggression problems. These dogs love to exercise, work, and play. Always on the lookout for something to herd, they'll happily settle for children if sheep aren't available.

Australian Shepherd	Collie
Bearded Collie	German Shepherd Dog
Belgian Malinois	Old English Sheepdog
Belgian Sheepdog	Puli
Belgian Tervuren	Shetland Sheepdog
Border Collie	

Collie

The Cattle/Sheep Driving Dogs

From the Herding group, these dogs were bred to drive sheep and move cattle long distances, often without man's direction. A hardy bunch, cattle/sheep driving dogs are more solidly built and stockier than the sheep herders. Athletic, dominant, and less predictable than their cousins, they need clear and consistent training. They are generally reserved with strangers and need early socialization to prevent aggression.

Australian Cattle Dog	Cardigan Welsh Corgi
Briard	Pembroke Welsh Corgi
Bouvier des Flandres	

Pembroke Welsh Corgi

Terriers

Losing is not in a terrier's vocabulary. Own a terrier and one word will spring out at you immediately—determination! They take a bite out of life and won't let go! There are two types of terriers: vermin hunters and fighting breeds.

The Vermin Hunters

These self-assured, spirited breeds are a lively bunch. Originally bred to listen for and hunt vermin on the farm, they are always on the alert and feisty when set to a task.

Agile and independent, they don't excel in off-leash training and need to be leashed when outdoors. If you're not a control freak and want a dog with spunk and good humor, take a good look at this list. Untrained or over-isolated, however, these dogs can become chronic barkers, chewers, or markers, and may develop aggression over objects and food.

Airedale Terrier	Manchester Terrier
Australian Terrier	Miniature Schnauzer
Bedlington Terrier	Norfolk Terrier
Border Terrier	Norwich Terrier
Cairn Terrier	Scottish Terrier
Dandie Dinmont Terrier	Sealyham Terrier
	Skye Terrier
Fox Terrier (Smooth and Wirehaired)	Soft Coated Wheaten Terrier
Irish Terrier	Welsh Terrier
Kerry Blue Terrier	West Highland White Terrier
Lakeland Terrier	

West Highland White Terrier

The Fighters

Originally bred to fight other dogs or to bait bulls, these breeds are cocky and courageous. Thankfully, they are no longer used for fighting and their combative instincts have been bred down. These dogs can make agreeable and entertaining pets. Early socialization and training are important—their pugnacious nature has been tamed, but not eliminated. Without this effort, fighting breeds can be dangerous around other animals, adults, and children.

American Staffordshire Terrier

Bull Terrier

Miniature Bull Terrier

Staffordshire Bull Terrier

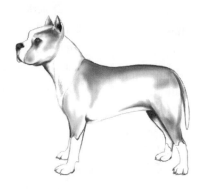

American Staffordshire Terrier

Grrr

Some slightly deranged people still think it's cool to watch dogs rip each other limb from limb. Although it's illegal, it still happens, so be very careful when buying one of these puppies. Make sure your breeder is breeding for mild temperaments only.

Non-Sporting Group

Many of these dogs were originally bred for specific work, but because dog work is hard to come by these days, they've become companions. Unlike other breed groups, there is little consistency in their personalities because they were all originally bred for different tasks. Before considering any of these breeds, consult breed-specific books and speak to a veterinarian to get a truer sense of what they are like.

American Eskimo Dog

Bichon Frise

Boston Terrier

Bulldog

Chinese Shar-Pei

Chow Chow

Dalmatian

Finnish Spitz

French Bulldog

Keeshond

Lhasa Apso

Poodle (Standard and Miniature)

Schipperke

Shiba Inu

Standard Schnauzer

Tibetan Spaniel

Tibetan Terrier

Finnish Spitz

Toy Group

Many of these breeds are miniaturized versions of working or hunting dogs. Too small to work, they have perfected the art of being adorable. Needing little exercise (although they definitely need exercise), they are perfect for apartment dwellers and older people. Playful and devoted, they demand constant affection and attention. It's easy to neglect training for these little guys, but it's a big mistake. Although small, they can become quite tyrannical, ruling the house with constant barking and snapping. To get the most from these precious companions, train them!

Affenpinscher	Miniature Pinscher
Brussels Griffon	Papillon
Cavalier King Charles Spaniel	Pekingese
Chihuahua	Pomeranian
Chinese Crested	Pug
English Toy Spaniel	Shih Tzu
Italian Greyhound	Silky Terrier
Japanese Chin	Toy Manchester Terrier
Maltese	Toy Poodle
	Yorkshire Terrier

A Toy Poodle clipped for the show ring

Mixed Breeds

Many people contend that mixed breed dogs are better than purebred dogs. I've owned both and have loved them equally. Love and loyalty know no pedigree. The biggest difference between a mixed breed and a purebred is predictability. When you throw a ball into the water for a retriever, you can predict what's going to happen next. If you know or can guess something about a puppy's background, you may be able to gain some insight into his personality. Like any other dog, a mixed breed needs attention, exercise, and training.

A friendly, garden-variety mixed breed dog

Chapter 2

Lifestyle and Litters

Are you a person with a busy social or work calendar? Dogs need lots of attention, especially when you're breaking them in or if they're pups. Just how much attention will be relative to the breed and the age, but all dogs need two to four exercise periods, two square meals, and a good block of love and attention every day. Certain breeds will need more interaction than others. Unlike guinea pigs or gerbils, dogs don't accept social isolation very well. You can't expect them to enjoy sitting in a room all day with newspapers and a bowl of water. But busy people need dog love, too! If you're an always-on-the-go type, choose an independent breed with a medium-to-low energy level *and make time in your schedule for your dog!*

Different Breeds and Their Energy Levels

Breed	Bred to...	Energy Level*
Pointers	Course fields all day, point, and retrieve	Very high
Retrievers	Stay by master's side, retrieve on command	High
Spaniels	Flush and retrieve birds	High
Setters	Run field, point, flush, retrieve fowl	High
Sighthounds	Pursue fast-moving game	High in spurts, then low
Scent Hounds	Follow and trail game	High
Large Game Hunters	Challenge large game	Medium
Sled/Draft	Pull sleds long distances/ pull carts to market	High/ medium
Guarding	Guard territory	Medium
Personal Protection	Protect home and master	Medium
Rescue/Water Dogs	Rescue humans	Low (Portuguese Water Dog = High)
Sheep Herders	Herd sheep	Medium to high

Breed	Bred to...	Energy Level*
Livestock Drivers	Move sheep and cattle from field to field	High
Terriers	Hunt barn pests	Medium to high
Fighting Breeds	Originally bred to fight each other or other species	Medium
Non-Sporting	All vary historically	Medium
Dalmatian	Currently bred for companionship	Very high
Toy Group	Companionship	Low

Energy Level	*Amount of Interaction Interaction Needed*	*How Often*
Very high	*20 minutes*	*2–4 times daily*
High	*15–20 minutes*	*2–3 times daily*
Medium	*10–15 minutes*	*2 times daily*
Low	*5 minutes*	*1–2 times daily*

Sarah Says

A tip for potential puppy purchasers: If your schedule is unpredictable, changing from week to week, you'll need to plan ahead for your new pup. New puppies need regular feedings and lots of outings when being house-broken. Older puppies can adapt to a more flexible schedule, as long as you don't forget a feeding.

If you're a work-at-home type, you (and your future dog) are in luck. Although your schedule can be complicated and hectic, you probably have the flexibility to pay lots of attention to the new arrival.

Fun and Leisure

What do you do for fun? Can a dog be included? Dogs don't like to be left out. And they're not choosy! Attending a soccer game, running in the park, sitting on your lap during a Garden Club meeting (small dogs only!)—it's all in a day's fun for your dog. It's lonely to be left at home. Some dogs can be very destructive if they feel deserted.

OOOH...

Doglish

Dogs left alone for an excessive number of hours develop *Hyper Isolation Anxiety*. When finally reunited, their tension is so high that they run around grabbing anything that'll fit into their mouths and jumping on furniture, counters, and people!

Living Quarters

Do you live in a big house or small apartment? Dogs need stretching room; the more energetic the dog, the more room required. Little dogs fit fine in big houses, but the opposite may not be true.

Also consider your neighbors. Some neighbors are less tolerant than others; if yours are the type who complain, you may run into trouble if you get a barker. Yes, they're a pain in the neck, but they're within their rights. The following table lists what living conditions are ideal for various breeds and how much each breed tends to bark.

Breed	Big House	Small Apt.	Prone to Barking
Pointers	✓	no	high
Retrievers	✓	no	medium
Spaniels	✓	with exercise	medium
Setters	✓	no	medium
Sighthounds	✓	with exercise	low
Scent Hounds	✓	with exercise	high
Large Game Hunters	✓	with exercise	low
Sled/Draft	✓	no	medium
Guarding	✓	with exercise	medium
Personal Protection	✓	with exercise	medium
Rescue	✓	with exercise	low
Sheep Herders	✓	with exercise	high
Cattle/Sheep Driving	✓	no	high
Terriers	✓	with exercise	high
Fighting Breeds	✓	with exercise	medium
Non-Sporting	✓	with exercise	varies
Toy Group	✓	yes	varies

Of course, there are always exceptions to the rule. This table considers the average dog in the group. Some are worse; some are better.

Lifestyle

Are you always flying off somewhere? Some breeds can't handle excessive kenneling. Jet-setters should find a breed that can. A few weeks here and there won't hurt. And don't forget that some hotels accept pets (hint, hint)!

If money's a little tight right now, avoid dogs that are high maintenance, such as those with pushed-in noses or skin flaps, who are naturally prone to health problems. Consult a veterinarian about the breeds you're considering before you settle on one.

Your Significant Others

In addition to your activity level, you need to consider the other people and commitments in your life. Are you single? Do you have kids? Are you retired? These things should influence your breed decision. Listed below are six *general* lifestyle situations. You might not fit perfectly into any one category—just read them over and keep that thinking cap on!

Single People

Single. Free. No commitments. Few responsibilities. Except one—a new puppy. You'll need to adjust your schedule around her. You'll need to socialize with her, take her out to meet your friends. If you work outside the home, consider a calm breed who won't need a five-mile run twice a day to be happy. Think ahead...a long way ahead. Where will you be in five years? Ten? No pressure here, but do you think you'll have kids? Think about a kid-friendly breed and take the time to familiarize her with kids while she's a puppy.

Couples

Do you both work? Can one be home enough to care for the new four-legged baby? The more attention she gets, the better. Puppies hate to be alone! You'll need lots of patience, tolerance, and perseverance. If you plan to have kids, puppies are great practice! You'll need to plan and share responsibilities. Someone needs to walk her, feed her, and socialize her. If you're considering a family, avoid protective, guard, and fighting breeds unless you're committed to early training and socialization with children and adults. If you both work all day, consider a more independent breed. You'll still be missed, but it won't be totally traumatic.

Children Younger Than Five

You already have puppies! Kids this small see puppies as playthings, so get a breed that can tolerate rough handling. I probably don't have to tell you that it's hard to teach a three-year-old not to pull and poke the puppy; it's important to find an accepting breed. You might want to consider an older puppy between 4 and 12 months old. If properly raised and socialized, an older pup will be calmer and less mouthy. Unless you're an experienced owner, avoid guard, protection, and fighting breeds. They are less tolerant of visitors and children.

Children Older Than Five

Kids over five can participate in a lot of puppy activities. Though you can't expect them to do all the work, they can learn a lot about responsibility through feeding, basic health care, and walking. If your kids are pretty rough-and-tumble, you'll need a breed that tolerates this. If your kids are past the rough-and-tumble stage (leaving for college, perhaps), you can consider many breeds. Again I caution you against protection, guard, and fighting breeds unless you're experienced and can make time in your schedule for extensive training. With doors flying open and kids running in and out, you want a kid-tested breed that can take it all in stride.

Retired People

This is a great time to add a dog to your family! Your schedule is probably a bit more flexible and you can be very attentive to your new pup. But remember, a puppy can be as demanding as a baby, so if you already did the diaper changing/4:00 a.m. feeding thing and don't care to repeat it, consider an older pup (between 4 and 12 months) who will have a head start on house training. If your retirement plans call for quiet walks and introspection, investigate the calmer breeds. If you intend to spend your retirement hiking and cross-country skiing, choose a breed that will complement your energy level.

Other Pets

Do you already have other pets? That will change the dynamics, especially if your other pet is a dog. Having a well-mannered dog to teach your new addition the ropes will make your life a lot easier. On the other hand, if your resident dog is a nut case, perhaps you should consider a little training before bringing another dog into your home.

Picking Your Breed

Now for the exciting part, picking your breed! I wish I could be there to help you in person, but since I can't, here's the next best thing: the questionnaire I give to clients who hire me to help them select the right breed. You'll find it in Appendix B. Don't worry—it's fun!

Once you've completed this little form, look it over and cross-reference your decisions to other sections of the book. You can also bring it to a dog professional (trainer or veterinarian) in your area, and ask him or her which breeds might be right for you.

Chapter 3

Somewhere, Out There, a Dog Waits for Me

In This Chapter

➤ When you should bring your dog home

➤ Finding a breeder versus going to the shelter or pet store

➤ How to pick your puppy out of a litter

➤ A temperament test to take with you

➤ Selecting an older dog

Dogs are a major responsibility! If you're reading this chapter, you're off to a good start. Though getting a dog is definitely one of life's most exciting moments, please read these pages carefully before you jump in head first. There are a few things, including a puppy temperament test, you should become familiar with ahead of time.

What's the Best Age to Bring Home a Dog or Puppy?

The best age to get a dog or puppy depends on one thing: whether you're getting a dog or puppy. If you're getting a puppy, the best age is between 8 and 12 weeks. If you're getting a dog, you may have a few surprises in store; old habits might need some correcting. So unless you're sure you've picked out a perfect peach, the younger, the better.

Grrr

If you're getting a puppy older than 10 weeks, make sure the breeder has "socialized" it by introducing it to everyday situations: people, sounds, and so on. An unsocialized pup may go to pieces around strange new things like vacuums, cars, or new people, and grow up to become a nervous dog.

Getting a Puppy

Many experts will tell you to bring a puppy home when it's between 6 and 8 weeks old, but I hold my "8-to-12 week" ground. Six-week-old pups nip and play in an early attempt to define a hierarchy. They even use mom as a biting bag, but she puts them in their place and teaches them respect. Respect is a good lesson for them to have learned before you bring them home. They're also just developing bladder control—waiting for a little more of that has benefits far beyond my casual explanation.

Getting a Dog

If you're getting a dog, you may have a few bad habits to deal with. This isn't a bad thing, but, at the same time, I don't want to leave you thinking all older dogs act like Lassie. Dogs are more set in their ways, like people. If "their way" jives with your lifestyle, then you're all set; if not, you may have some initial problems. For example, if you work all day and find an older dog who's accustomed to being left alone, you'll be set. If, however, you get a dog that has Hyper Isolation Anxiety or one who learned bad manners in his last home, you may have some big-time regrets when you come through the door of your home.

Here are some questions you should ask before bringing your dog home:

➤ How old is this dog?

➤ Has he had any training?

➤ How many homes has he had? If more than one, why?

➤ Does he have any bad habits, such as barking, house soiling, aggression, chewing?

I'm not arguing against love at first sight. Just know the cards you're dealt beforehand.

Finding a Reputable Breeder

If you're getting a purebred puppy, do me a big favor— find a reputable dog breeder. How? Ask your veterinarian. Contact the American Kennel Club at 5580 Centerview Drive, Raleigh, North Carolina 27606, (919) 233-3600 (or www.akc.org on the Internet), and ask for the address of the breed's parent club. The parent club will be able to recommend good breeders in your area.

Use good sense when visiting a kennel. Is it clean? How about the smell? What about the dogs—are they perky and friendly? A good breeder will have as many questions for you as you will for him. Don't be offended. Concern is a good sign. If the breeder is sloppy, the kennels are a mess, and the dogs are listless and poorly kept, you won't be able to trust anything he might tell you—from the pups' pedigree to their immunizations. Be sure to question the breeder's knowledge of genetic health conditions for your specific breed. A common example is hip dysplasia, which occurs in dogs ranging from 15 to 200 pounds. Hip dysplasia affects the proper development of the hip joint. Dogs prone to this condition should be OFA-certified before they're bred. Insist that your breeder shows you certification slips before you consider buying a puppy.

OOOH...

Doglish

OFA, the Orthopedic Foundation for Animals, rates dogs' hips as excellent, good, fair, borderline, or dysplastic (mild to severe) when they're two years of age. Make sure your puppy's parents have been certified and are over two years of age.

Here are some questions you can ask a breeder from whom you're considering buying a pup:

➤ How long have you been breeding dogs?

➤ Are the puppies socialized to unfamiliar sounds and people?

➤ Can I meet both parents?

➤ Is the purchase of the puppy guaranteed against health or behavioral defects?

➤ Have the parents been certified clear of genetic defects inherent to the breed? (You can ask your veterinarian what to look for.)

➤ Do you temperament-test the litter? If not, do you mind if I do so before selecting my puppy?

The ideal situation would be to find a breeder who is dedicated to the good temperament of the breed as well as the dog's conformation (the dog's physical characteristics compared to the ideals for the breed), who guarantees the puppy's health, and who is willing to let you temperament-test the puppies (if he or she hasn't done it) to ensure that you're ending up with a healthy puppy whose personality matches your lifestyle. When you visit the breeder, insist on meeting the mother dog and, if possible, the father dog. Their personalities leave their mark.

Sarah Says

Avoid buying any puppy who looks sickly, acts nervous or afraid, or who can't calm down after half an hour of interaction.

Pet Store Puppies

It's unbelievably cute, it's desperate, it looks so lonely, and it just went on sale—I'll take that doggy in the window!

Is this happening to you? If you're deliberating over a pet store pup, let me fill you in on the facts and then you can make your own decision. First, you have to know about puppy mills. Not every pet store gets their pups from these places, but some do, so it's best to be informed. Puppy mills are farms that breed dogs for profit, like chickens. If you haven't seen the pictures, let me tell you, they'd break your heart—cage on top of cage, row upon row, dogs getting little human contact and poor care…a pupomatic factory. Somewhere down the line, there is a price to pay for this neglect and it usually lands in the lap of the puppy buyer. Stress takes its toll on these little creatures; they often grow up to be nervous or distrustful. If you have a choice—pet store or breeder—you know where I'd place my vote.

If you find a pet store you'd like to buy a pup from, insist that the store prove that the puppy came from a breeder. Then call that breeder and ask the same questions for breeders listed in the previous section.

A Trip to the Shelter

Going to the shelter or checking the classifieds to find a dog can be depressing. You may see some dogs with limp tails and soulful expressions. There is a lot of love at animal shelters, so it's not the worst-case scenario, but it's still no fun for a dog who would much rather be curled up at someone's feet. No matter what, though, resist the temptation to take them all with you. Most dogs coming into a new home suffer from shelter shock and will need all your love and understanding to pull through.

Don't let all this talk scare you from your decision to rescue a dog from a shelter. It's the noblest of acts. I found the sweetest dog I've known at a shelter in Michigan and have never regretted it. But it is important to go to the shelter prepared.

OOOH...

Doglish

Abandonment isn't fun; abandoned dogs typically experience *shelter shock*. Sometimes it's for the best that the dog has a chance to find new owners, especially if he suffered from abuse or neglect, but a stay in the shelter is still hard on a dog's spirit.

Here are some things to keep in mind:

1. What physical and personality traits are you looking for? Small or big? Pup or dog? Calm or energetic? Make a list before you go and check with the kennel workers, who can be quite helpful and can guide you to puppies or dogs that fit your criteria.

2. Try to find out each dog's history. Most end up at the shelter with an excuse that their owners were

"moving" or have "allergies," but there's usually more to it than that. If a dog has been neglected or abused in any way, it may have behavioral problems you'll need to be prepared to cope with.

Sarah Says

If you adopt a dog from a shelter, count on having a behavior problem or two to iron out. Dogs who have spent any time at the shelter may need a refresher in the house manners department! The staff can give you an idea what to expect, but as the dog adjusts to you, more of his personality will emerge.

3. If you have children (or plan to have them), determine whether a dog likes them before bringing him home. Either bring your kids with you to the shelter to meet the dog, or borrow some!

4. If you have other pets at home, try to determine whether or not your candidate will accept them. Ask the shelter personnel if the dog was in a home with other pets or if he has had any exposure to other animals at the shelter.

5. Has the dog's health been checked? Are there any conditions (such as epilepsy or hip dysplasia) you should know about?

6. Walk the dog. Commune with him. Look into his eyes. Do you and the dog "click"? Is it love at first sight? I do believe in fairy "tails" (where dogs are concerned, anyway)!

Picking Out Your Puppy

You're on your way to see the puppies. You haven't seen the litter yet. I'm warning you, they're going to be unbelievably cute. This is the time to take a very firm stand: I am only taking one puppy.

So now you're peering into a box full of wriggling puppies. Chances are, one or two will capture your fancy right away. Maybe you'll like the biggest pup, the smallest pup, or the one with the most soulful expression. First impressions can be very persuasive, but you need to look at the puppy behind the pretty face before you make your decision.

Each puppy has a character all his own. Each will have his own way of approaching other puppies, interacting with you, and exploring his environment. You need to measure these qualities so you can see how the puppy's personality will complement your own.

Litter Line-Up

Dogs live in a world that's defined by a hierarchy, not a democracy. There's order in that world—it's just different from ours. If you want to impress your dog, think leader, Top Dog, alpha—whatever!

The Leader of the Pack

With Littermates: "Challenge and Win" is this puppy's motto. She loves to play and wrestle, mainly because she always wins. She thinks she's hot stuff and her behavior shows it. This is the puppy who is mock-fighting with the squeak toys and relentlessly attempting to break down the barricade.

With You: You'll probably meet her first. She'll charge forward, leap in the air, and wag her tail furiously. Don't get a swelled head—she's like that with everyone! This gal will mouth excessively, jump, and maybe even climb on top of you to show off her confident flair.

The Right Owner: Many people fall for this girl's greeting act. It's so flattering! But she's not trying to flatter you—she just wants to be first. Very intelligent and funny, she needs an owner with the time and perseverance to train her. Without a serious commitment to training, she'll become a tyrant and will make a difficult family pet.

The Next in Line

With Littermates: This puppy loves a good wrestle, too, and spends a lot of time fending off the Top Dog. When he's not under assault, he spends his time mock-fighting with lower-ranking pups and exploring his surroundings.

With You: Confident and happy, he's just not as pushy as the leader. He may mouth you and jump just to show you that he's a pretty outgoing puppy, too!

The Right Owner: Although not as cocky as #1, this puppy is energetic and boisterous and needs an owner with similar qualities. He'll keep a close eye on you and may take advantage when your back is turned. He's great with older children and a family dedicated to an assertive training regimen.

The Middleman

With Littermates: I call this puppy the explorer. She'll defend herself in a wrestling match, but competition is not really her cup of tea. She'd rather explore her surroundings and pursue more peaceful activities with littermates.

With You: What a relaxing change from the other two! She'll sit calmly, maybe getting up to follow you as you walk around the room. She might mouth or climb on your chest, but it will be moderate compared to you-know-who and her cohort.

The Right Owner: This dog is often ideal for laid-back families. She'll have a high tolerance for noise and confusion. Though she'll need training, occasional lapses won't result in a battle for control.

The Passive Pup

With Littermates: This puppy is shy with his littermates. He submits passively to the other puppies, who always know a softie when they see one. He interacts with lower-ranking siblings and enjoys quiet exploration and play.

With You: The passive puppy is calm and quiet. He might mouth you, but it will be pretty tentative. When you walk around the room, he may be more content to watch.

The Right Owner: This calm, considerate temperament needs an owner with the same qualities. Older children may enjoy this dog, but everyone must be aware of his sensitivity and use the gentlest handling techniques. This puppy needs training to enhance his self image, but it must done with much patience, very little discipline, and a lot of positive reinforcement.

The Shy Pup

With Littermates: Your heart will go out to this little creature. She'll show fear when approached by her dominant littermates. She may play with the other puppies, but will usually play by herself. This pup will be the one playing with a chew toy in the corner or exploring by herself while the other puppies are wrestling.

With You: You'll feel sorry for this puppy. She'll be happiest curled in your lap and may show fear if you make sudden movements or walk across the room. She won't like loud noises at all.

The Right Owner: The shy puppy is not good with children because loud noises and chaos send her into a state of shock. She'll need a very special owner who is patient and supportive. Gentle training methods will help to develop her self-esteem.

Puppy Tryouts

Now that you've taken a look at different puppy personalities, it's time to select your pup! The rest of this section presents seven exercises that you'll use to assess each puppy's personality. Perform each exercise with each puppy, and then rate each puppy's performance on the following Puppy Tryouts Score Card. (You can copy the card and take it with you as you visit various puppies.)

Test each puppy while he's awake and active. Perform each of the following activities with each puppy:

1. *Observe.* As they play with each other, observe the puppies and rate each one according to its rank in the litter. (It may help to refer to the earlier "Litter Line-Up" section.)

2. *Uplift.* After observing, take each puppy aside one at a time. Cradle him mid-body and suspend him four inches off the ground. If he squirms wildly and reaches out to mouth you, give him an A. If he squirms a bit but then relaxes, give him an N. If he shudders in fear or pins his ears back and tucks his tail, give him a P.

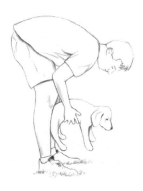

The Uplift test

3. *Flip-Flop.* Next, lift the puppy up and cradle her upside-down like a baby. Does she squirm and try to grab at you with her mouth? Give her an A. If she wiggles a bit and then settles happily, she gets an N. If she whimpers or pulls her mouth back in tension (a submissive grin), she gets a P.

4. *Gentle Caress.* Okay! Back to earth. Sit next to the puppy and pet him. Gently stroke him at least 15 times to judge his willingness to be handled. Does he immediately jump toward your face or scamper away toward a more stimulating distraction? Give him an A. Does he relax and sit quietly or climb in your lap? Give him an N. Does he cower, tuck his tail, pin his ears, or pull his mouth back in tension? Give him a P.

The Gentle Caress test

5. *Wacky Walk.* Stand up, shake your legs, clap your hands, and encourage the pup to follow you. Bend down like a monkey if you must, just do what it

takes to get her attention. Does she attack your legs or get distracted by a more interesting stimulation? Give her an A. Does she follow enthusiastically, looking up to your face for reinforcement? Give her an N. Does she sit and watch you quietly or withdraw in fear? Give her a P.

6. *What's That?* You'll need two spoons for this exercise. When the puppy is distracted, tap the spoons together above his head. If he jumps up and tries to wrestle the spoons, give him an A. If he ignores the sound or sniffs the spoons calmly, give him an N. If he cowers in fear or runs away, give him a P.

7. *Crash Test.* Walk at least six paces away from the puppy. Suddenly drop to the floor like you've fallen and hurt your knee. Don't get carried away, but make it look fairly realistic. Does the puppy take this as an invitation to play? Give her an A. Does she walk over and act curious? Give her an N. Does she run away or cower? Give her a P.

The Crash Test

Puppy Tryouts Score Card

Rate each puppy using the following scale:

A—Active (Top Dog and Next in Line)

N—Neutral (Middleman)

P—Passive (Passive and Shy)

Name/ Number of Pup	1. Observe	2. Uplift	3. Flip-Flop	4. Gentle Caress	5. Wacky Walk	6. What's That?	7. Crash Test

Letting Kids Help with the Puppy Testing

Young children can help out on the Gentle Caress and Crash Test exercises. In fact, it's a good way to see how your future puppy might get along with your current, less hairy "puppies." Older kids can do all of the tests, but only one test per puppy, please. If everyone in your family starts crashing to the floor, even the bravest puppy will head for the hills.

Tallying the Score

Now for a little score analysis. Count up your As, Ns, and Ps. Got it? If you're all As, I don't have to tell you what you're dealing with: a Leader type; one who'll want to take control if no one else steps up for the part! All Ns, and you have a Middleman on your hands. Ns and Ps mean your dog is likely to be a passive and easy-going. All Ps mean your dog may turn out to be shy without appropriate socialization. Identifying your pup's personality from the start will help you mold a training program that will be good for everyone.

Selecting an Older Dog

Selecting an older dog of any age can be a lot easier. The cute factor has lost its shine. You're usually testing one dog at a time, instead of 12. But if you have a bleeding heart like mine, a dog's individual story can suck you in even though the dog may be unsuited for your lifestyle.

So, to help you keep your head on straight, I've written some guidelines and a few tests you can set up if you're strong enough to let your head lead your heart. Nothing is sadder than rescuing a dog and having to return it because the dog couldn't cope with your life. Be strong—find out ahead of time by taking the following steps:

1. Do you have kids? Make sure you introduce them to the dog before you bring your dog home.

2. Startle the dog. Toss your keys on the floor. Does the dog fall to pieces or attack them? These are not good signs.

3. If you have an animal menagerie at home, make sure the dog can cope with creature chaos.

4. Ask one of the staff at the shelter (or the previous owner) to pick up the dog. What happens?

5. Bring a soft brush and try to groom the dog while feeding her treats. What happens?

Sarah Says

Sometimes people get purebreds from a breeder or even from a shelter. If you get a dog from a breeder, ask her to transfer your new dog's registration to your name. If you get a purebred dog from a shelter, you can take pictures of your dog and send them to the American Kennel Club. If they agree, they will offer your dog purebred status and provide you with a limited registration number, called ILP. Although you won't be permitted to show in conformation, this number allows you to show your dog in Obedience trials and compete in some other performance events.

Chapter 4

Rolling Out Your Welcome Mat

The day is arriving—it's time to pull out your plastic and do a little shopping for your new arrival! Although temptation may strike to buy every gimmick—from the latest toy to that designer doggy raincoat—I suggest you bring a list and stick to it. This chapter includes a sample list; the most important items are discussed next.

Your Shopping List

Shopping List for My New Dog:

❑ Crate

❑ Baby gates

❑ Fold-out pen

❑ Dog bed

❑ Collar

❑ Three bowls (two for water and one for food)

❑ Puppy or dog food

❑ Leash

❑ Dog toys

❑ Extendable leash

❑ Soft grooming brush

❑ Nail clippers

❑ Identification tag

Crates

The crate should be large enough to accommodate your dog when he's fully grown. Because some puppies may soil an oversized crate, buy one that has a divider available in case you need it. Ideally, the crate should be placed in a bedroom because both puppies and dogs hate being alone at night. If this is out of the question, place the crate in a well-trafficked room like the kitchen or family room.

There are two types of crates you should consider: metal or plastic. The metal crates are sturdier and allow better ventilation—definitely a must in hot environments. The travel kennels are made from a durable plastic and serve the same purpose. If you plan to air travel frequently with your dog, I'd suggest plastic. No dog should be left in the crate longer than six hours.

Baby Gates

Gates are a must to close off a play room (ideally the kitchen) and to block off forbidden or dangerous areas.

Leashes

We'll discuss training leashes more in Chapter 7. For now, purchase a lightweight nylon leash and an expandable lead, which you'll use for outdoor playtime and advanced training.

Bowls and Beds

If you're a decorator at heart, you'll have fun shopping for these things. Look hard enough and you'll find bedding to match every room and bowls to match the tiles in your kitchen!

Sarah Says

You don't have to break the bank on bedding! Most dogs are happiest curled up in an old sweatshirt or a towel. Some even prefer cool tile over soft and snuggly bedding. Feel free to improvise for this item.

Stainless steel metal bowls are best for food and water. They're completely hypoallergenic, they wear well, and are easy to clean. I suggest two bowls for water: one as a staple and one to keep by the toilet bowl to discourage bowl sipping. Have the bowls and bedding ready and in position before you bring your dog home. Put water in one dish and some treats in the other dish and in the bedding. What a cool surprise!

Food

Decide on a nutritional plan ahead of time. Dry food is best in the long run, though it may not be suitable for puppy's first few months with you. Consult your dog's breeder or ask your veterinarian or local pet supply store about your dog's or puppy's nutritional needs.

Collar and Tag

Have a buckle collar and tag waiting for your new arrival.
If you're getting a puppy, purchase a lightweight nylon
collar and a small tag. Don't worry if you haven't picked
out a name. A good tag should give your phone number
with a short message, such as "Please return me to 666-
555-4444."

When fit properly, you should be able to comfortably slip
two fingers under the collar. Check it often if you have a
puppy—they grow faster than you'd think.

Sarah Says

Call your local animal shelter and ask for
more information regarding tattooing or
ID chips. These quick and painless procedures are another insurance should your
dog get lost or stolen.

Toys

Be sensible. Resist the temptation to buy one of everything; too many toys will be confusing. Your dog will
think that everything mouthable is fair game. And please
avoid designating old shoes, socks, or other household objects as toys! You'll be sorry.

Hard bones are the best. If your plan is to use plastic or
gum bones, don't give your dog edible toys. He won't
settle for anything less. White, knotted rawhide can
expand in the stomach, so I don't recommend it. Puppy
pacifiers, gummy bones, hooves, or pig ears are safe.

The Trip Home

You've selected your one and only. The moment's arrived to bring him home! Unless it's a neighborhood litter, I'll assume you came by car. Now depending on the situation, the car ride can be quite an experience, so let me prepare you. Worst-case scenario: Your new dog gets carsick. It's a sorry sight, although there are a few precautions you can take:

➤ Have paper towels ready.

➤ Spread a sheet across the seat area prepared for your dog and bring a few clean ones just in case you need a change.

➤ Bring along a box for the puppy as you ride home. Boxes add a feeling of security. Place a towel on the bottom and bring extras in case your puppy gets sick.

➤ Bring someone along to sit with the dog, encouraging him to talk softly should the pup get nervous.

➤ Secure a light collar with an identification phone number (you can write it on the collar itself) in case you have an emergency or accident.

➤ Bring along a few chewies to divert the dog's attention.

➤ Drive slowly, taking each curve with care.

➤ Play some classical music and speak softly.

You may butt heads with some other nervous behaviors, such as whining, barking at passing objects, or eliminating. Stay calm. Don't correct your dog; it's a bad start and will only make him more anxious and homesick. Expect the worst, so no matter what happens, you'll be prepared.

Home Sweet Home

You've made it, somehow! All the anticipation has come to this very moment. The excitement level is probably up there, so take a few deep breaths. Too much tension can startle an older dog and may frighten a young puppy. I know you want to rush in and give your newest member the full tour, but hold your huskies! Remember dogs don't see their environment, they sniff it. Sniffing out an entire home might take hours and would be overwhelming. It's better to pick one room ahead of time, clean it, decorate it with dishes and bedding, and take the new pup or dog there initially. Share his curiosity as he checks out the room and speak to him sweetly. If your dog has an accident or grabs something inappropriate, don't correct him. He's too disoriented to retain anything so soon and you'll just frighten him. Relax! You're doing fine. This is just the beginning!

Are some of you wondering what you should do with the rest of your household? If you have some anticipating eyes waiting for you at home, the next few suggestions can help.

The Two-Legged Puppies

Talk about excitement. This day may be on a future "fondest memories of my childhood" list. However, it's your job to keep the kids calm. Too much squealing and loving in the first five minutes can be somewhat overwhelming for a pup. Explain the situation ahead of time and ask your children to help you make the dog or puppy feel comfortable. The rule is that they can follow quietly and speak gently, but all roughhousing, shouting, and fighting amongst themselves is forbidden. This may be your last peaceful moment for a while, so enjoy it!

Sarah Says

Don't overstimulate your new pal with 300 toys and millions of people. If he is enthusiastic and wants to explore everything, go with him. If he wants to sit in a corner all day, just mill around the room, petting him as a reward for venturing out. Don't pet him if he's cowering in a corner—you'll reinforce that behavior. If you pay attention to a timid dog, you'll have a timid dog.

Have a pow-wow! Gather everyone together and create a large circle by spreading your legs so your feet touch. Place the dog in the center of the circle and let him approach each person on his own. Discourage all unfair attention-getting ploys!

Other Pets

Don't expect your resident pets to be wearing party hats when you pull into the driveway. In all likelihood, they won't share your enthusiasm for the new family member.

Don't expect an older dog to jump with joy at the prospect of sharing his space with your new arrival.

The concept may take some getting used to. It's best to make the first introductions on neutral ground before bringing them together in your home. You'll probably see a lot of bluffing when the two first meet.

Don't interfere unless you see an unusually aggressive response—glaring eyes, drawn-back lips, and a growl that starts in the throat or belly. Some older dogs will growl or paw at a new puppy—this is a good sign. Big dog is showing little dog who's boss. Sometimes new dogs shriek if the resident dog even comes near; again, don't interfere! If you comfort the new dog, it may alienate your resident dog and make the relationship between them rocky. To keep the hierarchy harmonious, pay more attention to your resident dog, greeting and feeding him first. As long as he feels like he's still number one in your heart, he should cope just fine. It's hard not to meddle and feel protective of your newcomer, but remember, these are dog-pack rules!

Doglish

OOOH...

Bluffing, canine-style, can be recognized by showing the teeth, raised hackles, and shoulder pawing. It all looks pretty scary, but rarely escalates into a fight, so stay calm and don't interfere.

Cats have mixed feelings about new dogs. Some cats head for the highest object in the house and stare at you reproachfully. Some wait confidently for the curious dog to get close enough for a good, solid bat on the nose. In either case, keep your response low-key. Overreacting will make both of them nervous. If your cat can't come to grips with the idea, keep them in separate areas and bring them together when your dog is experienced with the Teaching Lead®, which is described in Chapter 7.

If there are other caged animals in the house, like ferrets or guinea pigs, don't bring them out immediately. Let the dog get used to you and then show him the cages when he's in a sleepy mood.

The First 24 Hours

The first day your new dog is home with you can be a little odd. After all the anticipation and preparation, your dog is home. Some dogs jump right into the swing of things; others prefer a more reserved approach. Don't compare your dog to others you've known and don't worry if he seems too rambunctious, too cautious, or too anything! This is all very new; he's trying to figure out what's going on. If he wants to sleep, let him sleep; put him in his crate (or sleep area) with the door open. At mealtime, put his food in or near his crate and leave him alone for 15 minutes. If he doesn't touch his food, that's okay. It's probably just his nerves! After the meal, give him some water and then walk him outside or to the newspapers (see Chapter 9 for more about this kind of training).

Ideally, your dog should sleep near you at night, in a large open-topped box or crate by your bedside (one he can't climb out of). He may whine the first few nights, but he'll feel a lot safer here than if he's alone in another room. If he whines, lay your hand in the box or on the crate. He (and you) may need to get up one to three times during the night to eliminate. Quietly take him to his spot and then back to his enclosure. Don't start playing games with the dog at 3:00 in the morning unless you like the habit. This topic is covered in more detail in Chapter 9.

If a bedroom is out of the question, crate him or enclose him in a small area, like a bathroom or kitchen. Turn off the lights, turn on some classical music, and be ready to walk him if he cries. Ahhh, the joys of doggy parenthood!

Your puppy can start out sleeping in an open-topped box by your bed so he can be close to you, but under control.

Chapter 5

You Can Be a Good Dog Trainer, Too!

SEE? LIKE THIS...

In This Chapter

- ➤ Who's to blame?
- ➤ Dogs have personalities too
- ➤ Understanding your role in the training process

A lot goes into being a good dog trainer and most of it's a mental thing. Even big dogs—dogs that weigh more than their owners—can be muscled or scared into good behavior. Dogs have spirits, just like the rest of us, that must be understood and encouraged in ways that make "dog sense." Your dog has bestowed upon you the highest honor, one you'd never receive from a human: a lifetime commitment to respect your judgment and abide by your rules. You need only to show her how.

Your First Lesson

The point of this section is to help you become a good dog trainer before you begin working with your dog. I'll go over stuff I'd teach you if I were working with you personally—stuff that will help you understand and train your dog better. There are four key things to remember.

A good dog trainer:

➤ Never blames the dog.

➤ Recognizes the dog's unique personality.

➤ Accepts and modifies his own personality.

➤ Understands his role in the training process.

Let's go through these one at a time.

Never Blame the Dog

Believe it or not, dogs don't react out of spite. Their behavior is directly related to their owner's reactions. My mantra?

A dog will repeat whatever gets attention.

They don't care whether the attention is negative or positive. So if anyone is out there saying, "I tell her she's bad, but she just ignores me!" I have something to tell you: Your dog interprets your discipline as interaction and will repeat the unwanted behavior again and again. Now I probably have you wondering how to handle unruly situations. Good. I'm whetting your appetite. The first step to becoming a good dog trainer is to stop blaming the dog!

Recognize the Dog's Unique Personality

Yes, dogs have personalities too! If you've had more than one dog, I'm sure you know exactly what I'm talking about. So many of my clients have started their sob stories with "My last dog was so easy…" "But," I respond with a smile, "this isn't your last dog. This dog is unique. And to train him, you must begin by understanding his personality."

Dogs Have Personalities Too

Based on my experience over the years working with countless numbers of dogs, I've noticed that most dogs fit into one of six character types. Identify your dog's character type and remember it as you work through the training chapters later in this book.

➤ *Eager Beaver.* These creatures will do whatever it takes to make you happy, though they can be difficult and manic if their training is ignored. They want to please so much they stick to whatever gets attention. If you like to toss the ball, they'll bring it back 500 times. If you encourage them to jump, they'll jump on you, and everyone else, whenever excitement builds. If you encourage them to sit and settle down on command, that's what they'll do. With this dog, all you have to do is decide what you want. There is no need to use harsh training techniques.

➤ *Joe Cool.* Laid-back and relaxed, they have control of every situation and seem to be less focused on you than their image. Give these fellows a command and they'll look at you as if to say, "in a minute," and then they'll forget. Organize a lesson and they'll fall asleep. Though they're quite funny and easy to live with, training is essential. Without it, they may not respond to you off lead. They may also be unmanageable in social situations. Diligent and patient training techniques are necessary.

➤ *Jokester.* I've owned a little comedian. A quick-minded perfectionist, Calvin taught me more about dog training than a lot of books I read. The reason? Comedians are revved-up wonder dogs who'll get into a lot of trouble if they're not directed. Dancing on the edge of good behavior, their biggest accolade is laughter and they must be firmly persuaded to cooperate. Laughter, after all, is attention—trust me, it's hard not to laugh at a dog prancing around with an oversized gourd in his mouth. Given clear, consistent, and stern instruction, comedians take to training well. Their puppyhood will test your patience, but they make wonderful dogs if trained.

➤ *Bully.* These dogs take themselves far too seriously. In a group of dogs, these dogs would have been destined to lead, and your home is no different. Unless you're experienced, dogs of this nature can be difficult to train. Aggression, physical leaning, and mounting are common. Training must be consistent and firm and should begin in puppyhood. If this is your dog, you must lay down the law now. Professional training may be needed. Do not proceed with training if your dog threatens you.

➤ *Sweetie Pie.* Docile and mild, these dogs like to observe situations rather than control them. They adore the people they love and must be trained under a soft hand. If you yell at them, or even at one another, they'll crumble. There is little to say against these dear dogs. It's easy to skip over training for them, but it's essential for their safety.

➤ *Scaredy Cat.* These dogs like to view the world from behind your legs. Soothe this behavior and you'll make it worse. Unlike children, who might feel relieved, soothing actually reinforces the dog's fear and makes it worse. You must act confident and relaxed in new and startling situations. Step away if the dog ducks behind you and only reinforce her if she calms down. Training is essential to help them feel more secure. These dogs respond best to a gentle hand.

Recognize Your Own Personality

Now it is time to analyze yourself. What kind of person
are you? Demanding? Sweet? Forgiving? Compulsive? Be
honest. Take out a pen and paper and write down three
adjectives to describe your personality. Now compare
them with your dog's character (identified from the list
of six presented in the last section). Are you demanding,
but your dog is a sweetie? Someone is going to have to
change. Making too many demands on a sweet dog will
frighten him. He'll shut down or run away when training
begins. If you're compulsive and you have a laid-back dog,
you'll be laughed at. Have you ever seen a dog laugh at his
owner? It's quite embarrassing. For you to be a good dog
trainer, you must modify your personality to suit your
dog's.

Understand Your Role in the
Training Process

One of my clients called me in jubilation one day. After
weeks of group training, she had figured it out. "Training
is about making the dogs want to work with you!"

In class, I repeat the same concept many different ways.
However, I understand that hearing the words and feeling
their meaning rarely happen simultaneously. Although
this student had listened to me, until this point she had
been training her dog by dictating her commands and
muscling through all corrections. She also carried out my
suggestions to the extreme: If I said to enunciate commands, she'd shout them. When I encouraged people to
tap their foot lightly to end a heel, she'd stamp it.

She loves her dog tremendously, but when she started
training, she was more obsessed with the mechanics than
the process itself. "Remember," I would tell her, "Dog
training involves two spirits: yours and your dog's. One

affects the other." To understand your role in the training process, keep these things in mind:

➤ Training is about making your dog want to work with you!

➤ Your dog isn't a machine; he's a spiritual being.

➤ You are your dog's leader.

➤ Every dog learns at a different rate. Frustration is catching, so stay calm.

➤ Your mom's right again—patience is a virtue.

Chapter 6

Not English, Doglish!

Until you can think with and not against your dog, you can't really train him properly. It's impossible for your dog to be human, no matter how much you work together. So how do you think like a dog? It's quite an adventure.

The Leadership Principle

Dogs have a lot of team spirit. This is often referred to as their "pack" instinct, but I like to think of it in "team" terms. Team consciousness and the canine psyche have a lot in common. Teams focus on winning; each player works for it, wants it, thinks about it, and strives for it. There are also some other, less obvious factors that determine a team's success. Three come to mind immediately: cooperation, structure, and mutual respect. Without these, even a group of phenomenal players would be pure chaos. A good team is organized so everyone knows who's in charge and what's expected from them. And should someone get in trouble or become hurt, he can trust that another teammate will help out.

Grrr

If you don't organize the team hierarchy, your dog will, and that can be a real nightmare. If your dog has the personality to lead, you'll be living in a very expensive doghouse under dog rule. If your dog doesn't have what it takes but feels he must lead because no one else has applied for the job, your house will be one big headache; dogs in this state are very hyper and confused.

Dogs live their entire lives, their every waking moment, by team structure. Instead of winning, however, their mantra is survival. And to personalize it one step further, you and your family are their team. For your dog to feel secure and safe, he must know who's in charge. It's your job to teach him what you expect from him in your home. Do you have more than one person in your household? In dogland, teams are organized in a hierarchy, so you must teach your four-legged friend that two-legged dogs are the ones in charge. This will take some cooperation on everyone's part, but it's very doable.

So how do you organize your team and teach your dog the rules? The first step is understanding what motivates your dog's behavior. Then you need to master his communication skills. It might sound like hard work, but it's quite fascinating. Your dog will respond to you more willingly if you make the effort to understand and learn his language. With an ounce of effort, a little time, and some structure, you'll earn your dog's respect, cooperation, and trust. Plus, you'll have a teammate who'll be at your side when the cards are down. You can't beat that bargain!

The Attention Factor

Dogs are motivated by attention. They live for it, love it, and will do anything to keep the spotlight focused on them. Does this remind you of a three year old? Well, add to this similarity the fact that they don't care whether the attention is negative or positive.

The Irony of Negative Attention

Though I'll address specific problems in depth in Chapters 10 and 11, I want to give you something now to whet your appetite! Picture a very excited, jumping dog. You're trying to read the paper calmly, but he wants your attention. What if you tried to correct the dog by pushing him down and screaming "Off!"? In all likelihood, the dog will jump again. Do you know why? Because you just gave him attention. Attention, in a dog's mind, includes anything from dramatic body contact to a simple glance. Yes, even looking at your dog will reinforce his behavior.

Does this blow your mind? Although it may sound far-fetched at first, it's actually pretty elementary. Dogs think of us as other dogs. If they get excited and then we get excited, we're following their lead. The fact that you might be upset with their behavior just doesn't register. Being upset is a human emotion. Excitement and body contact is a dog thing. Even if you push your dog so hard that he stops and slinks away, the only thing you've accomplished is scaring your dog. And who wants to train a dog through fear? Trust me, there's a better way.

Power of Positive Attention

When I ask my clients what they do when they catch their dog resting or chewing a bone quietly, most say, "Nothing. It's a moment of peace." I appreciate such honesty; however, that's when they ought to be showering their dog with attention. Not wild, twist-and-shout, hoot-and-holler attention, just calm, soothing, loving attention that makes them smile inside. A soft whispering praise is best, mixed with a massage-like pat. Remember my mantra?

Your dog will repeat whatever you pay attention to.

So you decide. What would you rather have? A dog that stays by your side with a chew bone or a frantic sock stealer that races around the house like a maniac? If you like the sock stealer, close the book. But if the bone-chewer image appeals to you, stick with me—we're going places!

Doglish

One more thing before we jump into the how-to's of training: I have to teach you the dog's language. To be the best teacher, you need to be fluent in Doglish. Give your family or friends a lesson too and encourage consistency.

Doglish consist of three elements:

➤ Eye contact

➤ Body language

➤ Tone

Words, feelings, and lengthy explanations don't count anymore. Complex reasoning is impossible for your dog to follow. Dogs are so innocent in their simplicity, it's beautiful.

Eye Contact

If you're constantly looking to your dog in stressful situations (someone's at the door or the dog's stealing the dish rag) and are having trouble encouraging your dog to pay attention to you, guess what? Your dog thinks you are depending on him to be the leader. He thinks you want him to make all the judgment calls. I know you're wondering how to handle these situations. In just a few pages, I'll tell you. But for now, understand that to train your dog, you must encourage him to look to you for direction. To leave you with an off-shoot of my attention statement:

You reinforce whatever you look at.

Look at a well-behaved dog and guess what you'll have?

Body Language

Body language is a funny thing. Imagine this...your dog becomes excited and hyper when company arrives at the front door. Desperate to save face, you start shouting and pushing your dog as the company is fending the two of you off with their coats. You try every possible command—"Sit, Boomer! Down! Off! Bad dog!"—but to no avail. The whole arrival scene is one big fiasco.

If your dog becomes excited and then you become excited, who's leading whom?

What's happening, dear readers? Who has copied whom? Whose body language has mimicked the other's? Are you feeling silly yet? Body language is an integral part of

Doglish. Play, tension, relaxation—they all have different postures. Going on the knowledge that your dog thinks you're a dog and doesn't quite grasp the "I'm pushing you frantically because I'm unhappy with your greeting manners" concept, what do you think you're communicating to your dog? You're the one who copied his body language. As you blaze the training trail, remember these three things:

> ➤ Stand upright and relax when directing your dog. I call this the peacock position.

> ➤ Don't face off or chase your dog when you're mad. To your dog, you'll look like you're playing.

> ➤ When trying to quiet or direct your dog, stand in front of him and stay calm.

Always remember, *you* set the example.

I hear two questions ringing throughout the pages already:

> How on earth can this be done?

> Can't I ever get down and play or cuddle with my dog?

We are getting there, and certainly you can get down and cuddle or play; that's one of the biggest perks in having a dog. But don't do it when your dog's in a mischievous mood or you'll be asking for trouble.

Stand up straight, relax your shoulders, and make eye contact. Peacocks rule!

Sarah Says

If you bend over when giving your dog a command, don't be surprised if he doesn't listen. You're doing the doggy equivalent of a play bow (a posture that invites a game). To put it in human terms, if you asked me to have a seat while you were hunched over looking at the floor, I'd think less of where to sit and wonder what on earth you were looking at. Stand tall and proud like a peacock when giving your dog directions.

Tone

If your dog thinks of you as another dog and you start yelling, what does he hear? Yes, he hears barking. And would barking calm excitement or increase it? Right again, it would increase it. Now some of you may have a dog that backs off from a situation when you yell, though he'll probably repeat the same behavior later. That's because yelling frightened him. He backed off because he was afraid of you, not because he understood. Yelling at any angle is just no good. So what works? Well, we'll get there in just a few moments, but before we begin, there are three tones you should commit to memory. I call them the three Ds:

➤ *Delighted tone.* Your praise tone should soothe your dog, not excite him. Find a tone that makes him feel warm and proud inside.

➤ *Directive tone.* Use this tone for your commands. It should be clear and authoritative, not harsh or sweet. Give your commands once from the peacock position.

➤ *Discipline tone.* I'm not much of a disciplinarian. My approach encourages more structure than strictness, but you should have a few tones that tell your dog to back off or move on. I use "Ep-Ep" a lot. The word doesn't matter as much as the tone. The tone should be shameful or disapproving, like "How could you" or "You better not touch that!" Discipline has more to do with timing and tone than your dog's transgressions.

As you can see, Doglish is quite different from English. Many people assume that their dog understands them when, in fact, he's often picking up the opposite message. If you chase your table snatcher, your English is saying, "How dare you," but your Doglish is saying, "PARTY!" Remember, every interaction you have with your dog gets translated into Doglish. From now on, you're being watched from a canine's eyes, so you had better start acting like one!

Grrr

Don't repeat your commands. Dogs don't understand words as words; they learn to respond to specific tones and syllables. If you say "Sit, sit, sit, Boomer, sit!" that's what Boomer will learn. If you want your dog to listen when you give the first command, make sure you give it only once and reinforce your expectations by positioning your dog.

Chapter 7

Collars and Leashes and Crates, Oh My!

SIT, TOTO, SIT.

In This Chapter

➤ Walking you through the pet supply store

➤ The training collar that's right for your dog

➤ Is there an alternative to crate training?

You've come to a pivotal point in your dog training journey. If you don't start out with the right equipment and make some effort to organize your home—I repeat, *your home*—you'll have a hard time earning your dog's respect. An untrained dog running free through the house, grabbing everything in sight, and pulling you all over the neighborhood is not a pretty sight. There's a better way.

It doesn't take too much to teach your dog the necessary skills for your mutual survival: a good collar, a few leashes, and a realistic enclosure system, both inside and out. Although you may feel the restrictions of such a structured lifestyle temporarily, you'll both be a lot happier in the long run.

The Right Training Collar

You can't simply ask for a training collar. You need to be more specific. There are many different types of collars available and finding the one for your situation is a must! An ineffective training collar can hurt your dog and/or hinder the training process.

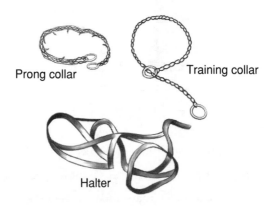

Training collar options

There are quite a few collars to choose from. Since I can't be there to help you determine which is most appropriate, you'll have to question a knowledgeable source if you're confused. Other trainers, veterinarians, or groomers may be helpful. Some dog people, however, are one-collar oriented; they'll tell you only one type will work. Shy away from that advice; every situation is different. What may work wonders for you could be someone else's nightmare. Choose a collar that works for you from those described next (try them all out if you have to).

The Original Training Collar

I call this the "original" because it has been around the longest. It has some other names too, like a chain or choke collar, although when used properly, it should never choke your dog. Choking and restraining only aggravate problems. It is the sound of the collar, not the restraint, that teaches. To be effective, you must put on the collar properly and master the zipper snap.

If put on backward, this collar will catch in a vise hold around your dog's neck and do what the collar is not supposed to do—choke! Take the following steps to ensure this doesn't happen:

1. Decide which side you want your dog to walk on. You must be consistent; dogs are easily confused. Because left is traditional, I'll use left as my reference.

2. Take one loop of the collar and slide the chain slack through it.

3. Create the letter "P" with the chain.

4. Holding it out, stand in front of your dog. Show him the chain.

5. Give him a treat as you praise him and slide it over his head.

Grrr

Do not use a training collar on a puppy younger than 16 weeks. Training collars should be used for teaching purposes only. Remove the collar when you leave your dog unattended because it can be deadly if snagged. Put your dog's tags on a buckle collar.

Master the zipper snap. Used properly, a quick snap (which sounds like a zipper) will correct your dog's impulse to disobey or lead. Try this without your dog: Stand up straight and relax your shoulders, letting your arms hang loosely at your side. Place your hand just behind your thigh and snap your elbow back so that you're swinging at the air behind you. Pretend my hand is there and you're trying to hit it. Now find your dog. Place your hand over the leash and snap back as he starts to lead forward. Touché!

If you find yourself in a constant pull battle with your dog that's only broken by occasional hacking, you might want to investigate other collar options, especially the self-correcting collar or chin lead.

OOOH...

Doglish

Adjustable collars made of cotton, nylon, or leather are called *buckle collars*. They do not slide or choke. Their purpose is to carry your dog's tags.

The Nylon Training Collar

For the right situations, these collars are a must. The rolled nylon collars work best on fine-haired dogs, whereas the flat style can work with any type of coat. These collars are a must for breeds with sensitive throats and can also be used with slow, cooperative dogs.

The "Self-Correcting" Collar

Yes, I know, it looks torturous, like a choke collar with large prongs. But it is perfectly humane (I promise), especially if you fall into the "I-can't-stop-choking-my-dog" category when using an original training collar (choke chain). This collar works on the quick external pinch-pain principle, which is less damaging than the constant choke of the chain collar.

Developed by the Germans for many of their bull-necked breeds, it works wonders for dogs who are insensitive to pain or too powerful to be persuaded with simpler devices. Though it's officially termed a *prong collar*, I refer to it as self-correcting because it requires little strength to use. By simply locking your arm into place, even the rowdiest of dogs will feel a pinch and slow down. It's no small miracle.

The "Chin" Lead

Once again, I have given an existing product a more descriptive name. Actually, this product comes in two forms. The pet supply stores sell a version known as a Halti®. The other brand is called a Promise Collar® and is sold exclusively through veterinarians. What's the difference? Price, color, and a fancy video, which is available when you buy the Promise Collar®.

Some of you may think this collar looks like a muzzle when you first see it. Trust me—it's not a muzzle; dogs can eat, chew, and play happily while sporting their chin lead. If I can take that a step further, it's probably the most humane way to walk a dog. It eliminates internal or external pressure around the neck, similar to a horse on a halter.

So how does this wonder collar work? It works on the "mommy" principle. When your dog was a pup, his mom would correct him by grasping his muzzle and shaking it. This communicated, "Hey, wild one, settle down!" The chin lead has the same effect. Left on during play, the pressure on the nose discourages rowdiness and mouthing. By placing a short lead on your dog when you're expecting company, you can effectively curb jumping habits. Barking frenzies are drastically reduced and training is made simple as you guide your dog from one exercise to the next.

For those of you who can look beyond its muzzle-like appearance, the chin lead is a safe, effective, humane training tool that will give you a leg up in correcting negative behavior patterns. Another plus is that leading by the chin demands minimal physical strength, so nearly everyone can use it—kids too! Here are a few more notes:

➤ *Wearing time.* How often you should leave the chin lead on is a question best answered by your dog! If yours is relatively well behaved, you can use it exclusively during training times. If he's the mouthing, jumping, or barking type, leave it on whenever you're around. Remove it at night or when you're out.

➤ *Sizing your chin lead.* Chin leads have a sizing scale. The chin lead must fit properly around your dog's neck. If it is too loose, your dog will pull it off and perhaps chew it. You want it to fit snugly about his ears, with enough room to fit two fingers under his neck. You may need to tie a knot with the remaining slack once you've fitted it to prevent it from loosening.

Sarah Says

If a chin lead irritates your dog's nose, buy some moleskin at the drug store and wrap it around the nose piece. It's softer and will feel more comfortable. If that's ineffective, remove the chin lead and contact your veterinarian for ointment.

➤ *Observe how your dog reacts.* Initially, dogs don't love the idea of a head collar. Their reaction reminds me of the first day my mother dressed me in lace—

I hated it. But after an hour or so, I hardly noticed it at all. I learned to tolerate it. So will your dog. When you see him flopping about like a flounder, take a breath. Once he realizes he can't get it off, he'll forget about it. Some take an hour and some take a day or two. If you want to give this collar a try, you may have to tolerate some resistance. Be patient.

No-Pull Harnesses and Other Gadgets

"There is nothing wrong with no-pull harnesses, although I don't recommend them professionally. They will prevent any pulling and give you a more pleasurable walk with your dog. However, *prevent* is the key word. They won't train your dog to walk next to you and may actually encourage more pulling when they're removed; for sled dog wanna-be's, when the leg contraption comes off, it's like being released from a chute—see ya!

Regular harnesses encourage pulling because they force your dog in front of you. With the exception of tiny breeds, I don't recommend them to anyone who has his heart set on a well-trained dog.

Gates, Crates, and Other Enclosures

You'll need to designate an area for your mischievous dog to stay while you're not home and to cool off if things get out of hand. I like to think of the area as a cubby because it should be small, quiet, and cozy. Don't worry, dogs like cubbies—it reminds them of their wolfish den roots. You can create a cubby by gating them into a small area or buying a crate.

Gates

Gates can be used to cubby your dog in a small area, such as a bathroom. Pick an area with linoleum or a tiled floor in case of accidents and be sure it's dog-proofed. Gates can also be used to enclose a play area. Kitchens make an ideal play area because they don't confine your puppy from you.

Use your gate to discourage your dog from entering off-limit rooms and to block off dangerous stairways and ledges.

Grrr

Do not use the crate if you're gone for long 8 to 12-hour days. It will drive your dog nuts. Isolated all day in a kennel, he'll learn to sleep during the day and keep you up all night. You'll create a nocturnal nightmare with the energy of six stallions, which is not good for either of you.

Crates

There are several different types of crates. Sizing is important. Crates come in two varieties: wire or mesh, some of which fold down nicely, or portable travel kennels made from polypropylene. Both do the job. If you're an airline traveler who wants to bring your pet along, I'd opt for the travel kennel. If you're a car traveler and want a crate that's easy to transport, mesh or wire crates are your best bet.

Crates are comforting for dogs who don't know how to handle open spaces and are especially useful for those pups having toilet training troubles. The size of the crate is important when you're housebreaking a dog or pup. If the crate is too large, the puppy may eliminate in one end and sleep in the other. If you have a growing puppy, buy an adult-size crate with a crate divider. Divide it so your puppy can lie comfortably and turn around only. Do the same if you have a big dog and a bigger crate. If no manufactured dividers are available, create one out of a safe, non-toxic material.

Crates can be an invaluable training tool, but they can also be emotionally destructive to your dog if overused. Crates are good in the following situations:

➤ When your dog must be left unattended for less than six hours

➤ During sleeping hours for young, unhousebroken, or mischievous puppies

➤ As a feeding station for distractible dogs

➤ As a time-out area for overexcited pups

There are drawbacks to using crates. True, your dog can't get into trouble there, but it won't teach him how to behave in your home. Isolation provides little training and has other drawbacks too:

➤ It doesn't communicate leadership.

➤ It separates you from your dog when you're at home.

➤ It can't communicate how to behave in the house.

Canine Playpens

Do you work all day? Consider the TIP Canine Playpen for your dog. This encloses your dog to prevent destruction while giving him plenty of room to stretch and move about. You can open it during work hours and fold it down when you're home.

When you leave your dog, go quietly, dim the lights, close the curtains, and turn on some classical music to encourage peaceful rest while you're out.

Leash Essentials

Ideally, your dog should be with you when you're home. But perhaps that concept has some of you shaking in your shoes. With all that unsupervised running around and destruction, your house will be trashed, your dog will be wild, and you'll be really sorry. Obviously, there's a better way: Keep your dog on a lead. Don't worry about keeping your dog on a lead in the house; it's only temporary.

You'll need to keep your dog secured for other reasons, too. The car comes to mind quickly. Keep your dog secured for his safety as well as your own peace of mind while you're driving. Romps too. If you're not in a confined area, it's unwise to let your dog run free. Let's take a look at leads, which are another training essential.

The Teaching Lead®

The Teaching Lead® is a leash, but not just your garden variety. It's a sturdy leather leash with lots of holes that's designed to teach your dog good manners passively. You'll use it to limit household freedom and structure situations so you can train your dog through positive reinforcement. Sound like a dream? Too good to be true? It's not. But before you take off, you need to learn and understand its three applications (which are explained further in the next chapter):

> ➤ *Leading.* You'll secure your dog's leash around your waist and lead him around using specific commands. Eventually, you'll be able to use these commands off-lead. Leading also helps you control your dog in stressful situations and allows you to make quick corrections when necessary.

My patented Teaching Lead® in action

➤ *Anchoring.* Anchoring is the process of sliding the leash around to your backside so you'll be able to calm your dog when talking on the phone or to company or waiting for your turn at the veterinarian's.

➤ *Stationing.* Select special areas for your dog in each room that you frequent. Decorate each area with a bed and toy. Initially, you'll need to secure your dog on a lead in a special area, but eventually you'll be able to send your dog there with a command like "Settle down."

The Short Lead

Short is relative to the size of your dog. A short lead should not be more than eight inches; for small dogs, one inch will do. My Seat Belt Safety Lead (SBSL)™ doubles nicely for bigger dogs. If you have a half-pint, buy a key chain and use that. Use this handy little device for two things: encouraging manners and off-leash training. Here's the theory behind both:

➤ *Encouraging good manners.* A lot of clients complain that their dogs behave like a saint on the Teaching Lead®, but when they take it off, the old derelict emerges. A short leash can serve as a nice transition from being on the Teaching Lead® to full-fledged freedom. Wearing it reminds the dog that you're still watching him and having it on gives you something to grasp for correction purposes if things get out of hand.

➤ *Off-lead training.* When we progress into off-leash work (yes, we are going to get there), the short lead again serves as a reminder. In addition, it gives you something to grab if your dog slips up.

The Flexi-Leash®

Flexi-Leashes® are fun, period. The longer, the better. Initially, they're great for exercising. Your dog can run like mad while you stand there reading the morning newspaper. If you feel like exercising too, all the better. You can quadruple your dog's workout. When we progress to off-leash work, the Flexi is a staple. Its tidy design works like a fishing reel, letting length in and out. Although it takes some coordination, once you've mastered it, you won't be able to live without it.

Initially, do not use it near roads or heavily populated areas. Its high-tech design takes some getting used to. Practice in isolated areas until you have the system down pat! If you're out with other people, watch their legs. Most dogs get a little nutty when finally given some freedom to run. If a person gets sandwiched between you and your dashing dog, he's in for a wicked rope burn! It's best to keep play times private.

Some dogs love to chew their Flexi. After all, the exercise and freedom are so exciting! Soaking the cord in Bitter Apple® liquid (purchased from the pet supply store) overnight can be a good deterrent. If this is ineffective, try snapping the cord into your dog's mouth. If the worst happens and the cord is severed, get a Phillips head screwdriver, open up the box, and sew the cord back together. It takes ten minutes and is cheaper than buying a new one.

Long Lines

I'll explain how to use long lines in later sections of the book. I don't want to overwhelm you now with the details, but if you're really organized and optimistic, you can create your own long lines out of a durable dog clip and rope (all of which you can purchase at a local hardware store) and put them aside for later. There are three:

➤ *The tree line.* You'll tie this line onto a tree to work on long-distance focus. Create or buy a 30-foot line.

➤ *The drag line.* Create or buy a 25-foot line.

➤ *The house line.* Create or buy a 10-foot line.

Outdoor Enclosures

Dogs need to be safely enclosed when allowed to run free outside. As I tell all my clients, "If you can't fence them, leash them." It's your responsibility to provide for your dog's well-being in the world, so think it through, talk to some educated folks, and make the right decision.

If you're lucky enough to have a yard, you should think seriously about enclosing at least a portion of it. Many people ask my advice about confining their pets using pens, tie outs, runs, or electrical fences; isn't it possible to just train a dog to stay on your property? Property training is not impossible, but it is not a safe idea. It takes a certain canine temperament and consistent training procedures over a long period of time. A dog that is property trained should not be allowed outside unsupervised.

The kind of enclosure you need differs in every situation. What kind of dog do you have? What's the dog's personality like? How do you want to use the fencing system; are you planning to leave your dog confined when you're not home or just when you're out with him? What kind of confinement would his temperament allow? How much property do you own? These are all very important considerations!

Pens and Tie Outs

Pens and chain link runner lines (RLs) designed to leave the dog unattended outdoors often create what I term Hyper Isolation Anxiety (HIA). Being social animals, dogs get anxious when left alone. This anxiety manifests itself in excessive barking, digging, destructive chewing, or frenetic activity when reunited with the owner. Runner lines are only beneficial if the owner remains with the dog and focuses him on exercise games. Keep in mind that the dog must be leashed when taking him to his confinement area; otherwise, he may bolt.

Full Yard Fences

Enclosing your entire property is a great option for many dogs. This enclosure enables them to enjoy their freedom and accompany you on your outdoor tasks. You can install a doggy door so your dog can monitor his own comings and goings between the house and yard. Unfortunately, full yard fences have their drawbacks too. If the dog is left alone for prolonged periods of time, this enclosure also can create HIA. Given close access to the house, some dogs may chew the base boards around the entrance door or the welcome mat. Dogs prone to digging can also escape quite easily. Hounds, Nordic, Sporting, and Terriers are just a few breeds famed for their acrobatic escapes! It only takes one escape to lose your dog to a tragic occurrence.

Electric Fences

One option growing in popularity is the electric fencing system. This seemingly magical creation keeps dogs enclosed by an underground wire that creates a shock when a dog wearing a battery-powered collar approaches. It's the ideal system for dogs who habitually dig and love to run, as long as the dog is otherwise properly trained. *But remember, dogs can get through this fence.* The best guarantee is proper and patient training.

Grrr

Collars that transmit the stimulus are battery-run. You'll need to check the battery and replace it approximately every six weeks.

Chapter 8

Bricks and Mortar: Getting Started

In This Chapter

➤ Using the Teaching Lead® in place of the crate

➤ Encouraging good household manners

➤ Teaching your dog to "settle down"

➤ Laying a proper foundation for training

The first thing you must accept is that your dog really doesn't know too much. She's willing to learn, but until you follow a good training regimen, she probably won't respect your rules. The complexity of the human household—the furnishings, the walls, the counters, the garbage pail—doesn't mean much to your dog. Don't worry, though. She'll understand soon enough!

Teaching involves communication. You must convey your expectations in a way that gets through to your dog. Remember, dogs aren't human. Lengthy explanations aren't going to impress her. You'll have to be a little more inventive. Need help? Let me share with you a little invention of mine called the Teaching Lead®.

Working with the Teaching Lead® (or a Reasonable Facsimile)

The Teaching Lead® is a leash designed to communicate control and condition appropriate household manners without discipline or force. Have I piqued your interest?

Here's what else the Teaching Lead® can do:

➤ Take the place of the crate when you're home

➤ Help you house train your dog

➤ Eliminate excessive jumping and counter sniffing

➤ Encourage appropriate chewing habits

➤ Discourage nipping

➤ Calm your dog around company

The Teaching Lead® unveiled

Sarah Says

Leather leashes provide better leverage while training your dog. I've always insisted on leather for my Teaching Lead® and have been complimented on its sturdiness. If you have a chewer, protect your leash with Bitter Apple® (available from pet supply stores) or Tabasco sauce.

And this is just the tip of the iceberg. There are many hidden benefits to using the Teaching Lead®. The best thing about it is that it's completely dog-tested, veterinarian-approved, and user-friendly!

You can make your own by buying a sturdy leather lead and simply tying it around your waist—it's equally effective.

The Teaching Lead® can't be bought in stores, but I've patented it and made it available through the order form in the back of this book. Its attractive and innovative design enables you to quickly clip the dog from your waist to immovable objects without fuss.

It's a solution that allows you to keep your dog with you and hang onto your sanity. The Teaching Lead® has three applications: leading, anchoring, and stationing. I'll describe each of these next.

Leading with the Teaching Lead®

This is the most humane training technique out there and it's not as hard as it sounds. Leading involves securing your dog to your side and leading her around the house using specific commands. (Once she understands this, you can extend your control outside.) Eventually, she'll respond to you off-lead. However, right now, she needs some direction.

Leading

Here's how to lead with the Teaching Lead® or a fac-simile:

1. Make sure you are using the right training collar. (Remember, until your puppy is 16 weeks, use the regular buckle collar.) Please review Chapter 7, if necessary, to find the collar best suited to you and your puppy.

2. Slide the leash around your waist like a belt. Put the clip to your left side if you want your dog on the left or your right side if you want him on your right. Everyone who walks your dog must keep him on the same side (do not have one person walk him on the left and another on the right). Connect the end clip to the appropriate waist hole and you're ready to begin!

3. To teach your dog proper leash manners and pre-vent pulling, take your dog to a hallway. Walk straight ahead, but watch your dog.

4. The second he walks ahead of you, call out his name as you pivot and dart in the opposite direction. Praise him, even though you may have pulled him. Continue to turn away from him until he pays attention to his name and stops trying to race ahead.

5. Now you're walking in style! Where you lead your dog must follow. This is your big chance. All household decisions are up to you. It may seem awkward at first, but soon you won't even know he's there. You might even call it fun! Remember, you're teaching your dog to follow you, so if there's a conflict of interest (he wants to go left when you're going right), go *your* way and encourage him to follow.

Sarah Says

Gauge your darting style for the dog's size. Do you have a monster? Dart big. A little guy? A strong step will do.

6. As you lead your dog around, start using commands conversationally. Encourage everyone around your dog to use them, too. Speak clearly, give your commands once, and enunciate your syllables; dogs understand sounds, not words. Here are five foundation commands to get you started:

    -   *"[Name], let's go!"* Give this command whenever you start walking or change direction. As you turn, hold your head high and don't look at your dog until he's turned with you.

    -   *"Sit."* Use this command whenever you offer your dog something positive like food, praise, a toy, or a pat. Say the command once, helping him into position if he doesn't respond.

The most important rule of thumb is, say "Sit" once only! Dogs understand sounds; "Sit-Sit-Sit" sounds much different than "Sit."

- *"[Name]."* A few times each day, stand in front of your dog proud and tall (remember the peacock?) and call out his name. If he doesn't look up immediately, direct his eyes toward you with a finger and a fun clucking sound.

- *"Wait"* and *"OK."* This duo is a real prize. Imagine getting your dog to stop before he races downstairs or across thresholds. Each time you're crossing a threshold or heavily trafficked area, command "Wait," and bring your dog behind you with his lead. He may get excited, but wait until he settles down before you command "OK." Make sure your feet cross the threshold first. Leaders must lead!

- *"Excuse me."* Use this whenever your dog crosses in front of or behind you. Also use this if your dog presses against you or blocks your path. As you say "Excuse me," gently knock your dog out of your way. Remember, dogs respond to hierarchies, so you need to establish yourself as the leader.

If you feel like taking a break, you can do two things: have interactive play time in an outdoor enclosure or using a Flexi-Leash®, or station him as described later in this chapter (make sure his bladder is empty). There will be days when you station much more than lead—that's okay. Use both methods interchangeably, but keep that dog with you when you're home!

Everyone who can lead the dog around should! You don't want your hierarchy to become a dictatorship. The only unacceptable combination is small children and big puppies. Other than that, everyone should take part. If the lead is too long for a child, she can wear it like a banner across the chest.

Grrr

Some dogs love to walk their owners. It's enormously fun and reminds them of all those tug-of-war games you play together. The first step in correcting this problem is eliminating those tug-of-war games. When your dog takes the leash in his mouth, snap it back *into* the roof of his mouth (not out of his mouth) sharply and give a firm "No!"

Some dogs like to imitate *mules*. It's a passive form of resistance. Your dog is hoping that you will rush back and give him lots of attention, but please don't. There are two approaches to discourage this, depending on the dog and the situation.

➤ *Keep trucking.* Don't turn around! Praise the air in front of you and walk a little faster. When your dog catches up, praise him happily and continue. This method works well with large breeds who have a reputation for being stubborn.

➤ *Kneel forward.* If you have a more delicate breed or a dog with a timid temperament, kneel down in front of him when he puts on the brakes. Tap the floor and encourage him to come to you. When he does, praise him warmly, then go to the end of the leash again and repeat yourself. He'll catch on soon. Remember, no attention for stubborn stopping and absolutely no pick-ups!

Letting your dog run free in your house before he's trained can be a big mistake. He'll run wild, you'll chase him, and the whole thing will be remembered as one big game! He'll think dogs lead and people follow. Instead, leading will give you the upper hand. Your dog will learn to follow your lead and you'll be able to quickly discourage all inappropriate behavior and reinforce the good stuff!

Anchoring Your Dog

As you're leading, you may need to sit down to talk on the phone, do homework, talk to the plumber, or whatever. If you let your dog free at such a point, he might create havoc in his constant quest to get your attention. Jumping on the counter or chewing the drapes can be real eye catchers, even when your attention is elsewhere. Instead of these habits, I advise you to create a more civilized routine. I call it *anchoring*.

Anchoring helps your dog learn to lie down.

With your dog secured to your side, slide the end clip around to your tail bone and sit on the remaining slack of the leash. Leave enough room for your dog to lie comfortably behind your feet and offer him a favorite bone to keep him occupied. Pet and praise your dog when he settles down or chews his bone.

Stationing Your Dog

Stationing gives you the freedom to take your dog into each room of the house and show him how to behave there!

Stationing gives your dog an area to take it easy in.

To station your dog or puppy, you'll first need to select your areas. Go into each room you'd like your dog to behave in. Pick a good area for him to settle in—perhaps one near the couch in the TV room, but away from the table in the dining room. This will be his station. Eventually, he'll go there automatically. Right now, you must secure him on a lead.

Decorate each station with a comfy cushion or blanket and a favorite chew toy. This will help your dog identify his space. Ask your veterinarian for suggestions. Avoid rawhide bones with big knots—they can cause indigestion and other problems. Remove end fragments of hooves or rawhide to discourage gulping.

Use a product like Bitter Apple® to discourage your dog from test-chewing the surrounding furniture or rugs. You can find it at your local pet supply store.

Initially, tie your dog at his station until he learns his place. Wrap the Teaching Lead® around an immovable object and attach the top clip to the opposite end of the leash. Alternatively, you can screw an eye hook into the wall and clip the leash through it. When stationed, your dog should have no more than three feet of freedom; given too much room, he may piddle or pace.

If your dog chews on the leash, you can discourage him by rubbing Bitter Apple® on the leash. It's vile-tasting, but harmless. If Bitter Apple® is not effective, you can try a home-cooked mixture: some red pepper juice with a little garlic or Tabasco sauce. If all else fails, get a chain lead and temporarily station him using that.

Sarah Says

Your dog wants to be with you or another family member whenever you're around. The point of stationing is to teach him how to behave in social situations, so make sure you station him in a room with people.

If you must leave your dog, tell him to "Wait." Short de-partures are good because they get your dog used to being left alone and show him that you won't desert him. Go calmly. If he's excited when you return, ignore him. You don't want to reinforce that. When he's calm, give him attention.

When first practicing the stationing procedure, stay with your dog. Make him feel comfortable in the area and encourage him to chew his bone. Leave him only when he's busy with a chew toy or resting.

Grrr

Some dogs panic when initially stationed. If you're concerned, determine whether your dog's reaction is really a panic attack or simply a persuasive protest. Ignore the protest. If he is truly panicked, initially station him only when you can sit with him. Encourage bone chewing and begin to leave his side only when he's sleeping. Pretty soon, he'll get the hang of it.

Bravely ignore whining or barking, unless your dog's communicating a need to go out. If he barks and you soothe him, you're teaching a lesson with headache written all over it. You may try distracting your dog by using a fancy long-distance squirt gun. (I found the Super Soaker to be very effective—long range and accurate, too!) But you must be very sneaky; he can't know where the water is coming from. Only release a dog from a station once he's calm and quiet.

As you lead your dog to his station, give the command to "Settle down" and point to his spot.

WARNING TO PUPPY OWNERS: Puppies can't handle being stationed too long. How long will depend on the age and mental state of your pup. A sleepyhead of any age can handle an hour or more. An older pup can handle more extended periods. The best gauge is your puppy; keep him stationed near you and be aware of his signals. If your pup has been napping at his station for an hour and suddenly gets up and starts acting restless, it's probably time to go to his bathroom spot. If your puppy chews on a bone for 15 minutes and then starts acting like a jumping bean, it's probably an energy spurt and time for a little play.

Other guidelines for stationing pups and older dogs:

➤ Your puppy must be at least 12 weeks old before stationing.

➤ Make sure the station is away from stairs, electrical cords/outlets, or entanglements like posts.

➤ Be sure the object you attach the dog to is immovable and sturdy.

➤ When securing your dog, attach the clip to the buckle or tag collar, never a training collar.

Chapter 9

Housebreaking

In This Chapter

➤ Structure, structure

➤ A simple routine

➤ Words to memorize

Dog doo on the carpet is perhaps one of life's more wrenching sights. I hear the following quote daily from my clients: "She knows it's wrong! Just look at her eyes; guilt's written all over her face."

No it's not—dogs don't feel guilt. They really don't. You might be noticing fear and confusion, but after-the-fact corrections won't help your long-term goal. If you have a housebreaking problem, you need to accept that your dog doesn't know much about your home. Approach this project with a level head. Your dog isn't human—never will be—but, fortunately, she can be potty trained to go outside or on papers. Here's how.

Sarah Says

Use a word like "Outside" as you lead your dog to her potty area.

The Outside Routine

The most important aspect of housetraining is establishing a routine, as follows:

1. *Select a spot.* Pick an area to potty train your dog. If it's outdoors, you must take your dog there before you walk him.

2. *Blaze a trail.* Be consistent. Follow the same path to your dog's area each time you potty her. Use the same door.

A structured routine is a must!

3. *The attention factor.* Don't greet or praise until after your dog has pottied.

4. *The command.* As your dog is eliminating, say "Get busy." Eventually, he'll go on command. It's no small miracle.

Grrr

Do you have a small dog or young puppy? Don't carry him to his area. Let him walk so he can learn how to navigate on his own.

5. *The reward.* Once he has pottied, greet, praise, and walk him as usual!

Your pup will need to go after feeding, exercising, napping, and isolation. Use the following table as a guide.

How Many Times a Day Your Dog Will Need To "Go"

Age	Trips to the Spot
6 to 14 weeks	8 to 10
14 to 20 weeks	6 to 8
20 to 30 weeks	4 to 6
30 weeks to adulthood	3 to 4

Lay Off Corrections

Getting mad makes you look foolish. You're getting mad at a dog. As much as you think she's human, she isn't. Even though I've heard it a thousand times, I'm still not convinced that "dogs understand." You can interrupt the process if you catch it, but lay off all other corrections.

Interrupting the Process

If you catch your dog in the process of eliminating in the house, startle her. Clap your hands as you say "Ep, Ep, Ep!"; jump up and down like an excited chimp—whatever it takes to get her to stop. Then direct her to the elimination area like nothing happened. Praise her for finishing.

Keep Your Dog Confined

Use your Teaching Lead®. Crate your dog when you're out and at night, if she's not stationed. You'll be able to grant her more freedom after she learns the rules, but not now.

Keep the Diet Consistent

Avoid changing dog food brands unless directed to do so by your veterinarian. Dogs don't digest the way humans do. Their stomachs can get upset if you change their diet. Lay off treats for a while until they're housebroken.

Watch Water Intake

Dogs, especially young ones, drink water excessively if they're bored or nervous. If your dog is having peeing problems, monitor his water intake by giving him access during meal times and as you take him to his area. Be careful not to dehydrate your dog. If he looks thirsty, let him lap! Remove water after 7:30 p.m. If he needs a drink, give him ice cubes, which absorb faster into the bloodstream.

Learning Your Dog's Signal

Once you have the routine down pat (give it about a week), interrupt it. Instead of chanting "Outside," lead your dog to the door. Wait until she gives you a signal to continue. If her signal is subtly staring at the door, call her back to you and pump her up, "What is it? Outside? Good dog!" and out you go. Repeat the process in rooms farther and farther from the door or her papers.

Puppy Considerations

Puppies need to go out more frequently than older dogs. Really young puppies, younger than 12 weeks, may need to go out every hour or two. Believe it or not, there is a pattern to their elimination habits. Puppies go after they sleep, play, eat, and after long bouts of confinement. Be patient. Some train in days; others take months.

Still Having Difficulty?

If you're still having problems, go through this checklist to ensure you're doing everything by the book.

- ✓ Limit your dog's freedom unless he just pottied in the right place and you can watch him 110 percent.

- ✓ Crate or isolate your dog when you're out.

- ✓ Use the Teaching Lead® to keep your dog with you when you're home.

- ✓ If your dog eliminates when stationed, you may be giving him too much freedom. Two to three feet is appropriate, depending on the size of your dog.

- ✓ Are you giving the dog attention before she eliminates? Wait instead and let the dog earn your love by eliminating in the right place!

- ✓ Give your dog five minutes to do her business. If your dog lingers, crate her for 15 minutes and start from the top.

- ✓ Are you following a consistent routine and encouraging everyone to do the same? Consistency is key!

If you're still having problems, seek a professional animal trainer or behaviorist. Good guidance will leave you wondering why you didn't opt for it months ago!

Chapter 10

Other Horrors

In This Chapter

➤ How to curb nipping, chewing, and barking

➤ When your dog's idea of fun isn't fun for you

➤ Four paws on the floor: Redirecting your jumper!

Order in the house! Order in the house! Sometimes you'd like to yell it and have it be so. Teaching household etiquette may be the most trying time for you and your dog. While your dog is trying to figure out what you want, you've been reduced to pleading for cooperation: "I'll give you a biscuit. Biscie, Boomer? Please, Boomer, please? I'm late for work."

It's embarrassing. You need some guidelines to get on the right track. In this chapter, I'll cover chewing, the infamous grab-n-go, jumping, barking, and nipping. (The more serious infractions will be covered in the next chapter.)

Stop Chewing!

Chewing is a dog thing. It's nothing personal. They don't know a stick from furniture or a doll's head from a chestnut. Fortunately, they can be rehabilitated. If you have a habitual chewer on your hands, however, you'll need to be patient and use some of the tried-and-true techniques described next.

Buy Stock in Bitter Apple®

Bitter Apple® is nasty-tasting stuff you can buy at most pet supply stores that you can spray on items to prevent your dog from chewing them. If you notice your dog chewing on the furniture surrounding her station, spray everything but her bed and bone. Believe it or not, some dogs like Bitter Apple®. If this is your dog, try a Tabasco sauce mixture.

Provide One Main Toy

Having too many objects to choose from can confuse your dog. Pick a bone or toy that will satisfy your dog's penchant for chewing, buy multiples of that item, and spread them around the house for quick access. Do the same for play toys.

Avoid Prize Envy Confrontations

Don't yell at your dog after she's begun or after she's finished chewing. It's too late. If you chase a dog who has something in her mouth, she'll be thinking, "Wow, what a great prize...everybody wants to take it from me!" (This is called prize envy.) Instead, learn about the treat cup and use it effectively.

Making a treat cup is easy. Break up your dog's favorite treats in a cup. Shake the cup and offer your dog a treat. Continue this until your dog associates the sound of the cup with getting a treat. Now spread treat cups all over your home.

Any time your dog is chewing on an acceptable object, go over with the treat cup, say "Out," offer her a treat, and leave. When your dog's eating a meal, shake the cup, say "Out," offer her a treat, and leave. Now that you've communicated that your approach is not threatening, the next time your dog grabs something, find a treat cup and say "Out." Treat all objects she grabs, good or bad, as treasures and she'll be much more cooperative. Praise her when she releases the object and help her find a chew toy: "Where's your bone?"

If It's Gone, It's Gone

If your dog has destroyed something, let it go. Yelling or hitting your dog will only make him nervous and frightened, which leads to more chewing. Any dog owner can commiserate (and I know firsthand how angry you feel), but don't take it out on your dog. He doesn't know any better. Remember, your dog's mouth is equivalent to your hands; if your dog is nervous or fidgety, he'll chew. I'm sure if your dog could surf the Internet, scan the soaps, or pull his hair out, he would. But since he can't, chewing will have to do.

Catch Your Dog in the Thought Process!

Set up a situation with something your dog's obsessed with—tissues, shoes, a Barbie doll, whatever. While your dog's resting in another room, set the object in the middle of the floor and bring her to it on her Teaching Lead®. The second your dog notices the object, say "No," and snap back on the leash. Next, pick up the object and shout at it. You read right. Get angry at the object, not your dog. You're doing the dog version of telling a child the stove is hot. Now walk by the object again. Your dog should avoid it like the plague. Use this technique to catch your dog in the thought process; if your dog already has an object in her mouth, you're too late.

Still Having Trouble with Your Chewer?

If you're still having problems with your dog chewing, go through this checklist to ensure you're doing everything by the book. If you're following the list but are still having problems, call a professional.

✓ Limit your dog's freedom around the house until she's a respectable chewer.

✓ Avoid the infamous "grab-n-go." This is when your dog grabs an object just to get you to chase him. It has dog-fun written all over it. Decide on an alternative game plan and teach everyone to follow the same routine.

✓ Don't yell at your dog after the fact. She'll consider your aggressive interest a sign that whatever she's found must be valuable because you're willing to challenge her for it.

✓ Treat cups and discipline don't mix. Treat cups encourage your dog to show you her treasure. Don't correct her (or the object) after she's given it up or she won't bring it to you again.

Jaws Junior: Nipping and Mouthing

Mouthing and nipping are two different issues. *Nipping* is a puppy thing; it's interactive and playful. *Mouthing* is a lesser infraction; it's more of a communication skill to get you to do something. Less pressure, less annoying, but still not a charming habit. If you have an older dog who still nips, read the section on aggression. Nipping dogs are bossy and manipulative and need a firmer regime.

Grrr

Dogs interpret discipline as confrontational play. Excessive physical corrections will result in aggression. Be wise; stay cool.

Mouthing is an attention-getting behavior. If your dog uses it to communicate a need to go out, respond. If your dog is mouthing you for a pat, please ignore it. Pretend she isn't there. If she becomes too annoying, get some Binaca Breath Spray® and spritz her discreetly, hiding the Binaca in your hand, avoiding all eye contact, comments, or pushing.

Nipping with sharp little needle teeth can hurt! It's another one of those dog things that you'll need to refocus. Consider this: When your puppy still hung out with her littermates, she nipped during play and to determine her rank. She also soft-mouthed her mother affectionately. When you bring your puppy home, what happens? This behavior continues. What your puppy wants to know is, who's a puppy and who's not? This determines the type of mouthing or nipping: soft or playful. Usually, everyone gets categorized as a puppy. Why? Well for starters, most people pull their hand away when nipped. To a human, it's self-defense. To a pup, it's an invitation to play. Even if you were to correct your young puppy, she wouldn't get it; it's like correcting a one-year-old baby for pulling your hair. So what should you do? Good question. Your approach will depend on your puppy's age.

Younger Than 14 Weeks

Young puppies mouth a lot. They mouth when playing; they also mouth to communicate their needs, just like a baby cries. If your puppy starts mouthing, ask yourself: Is she hungry or thirsty? Does she need to eliminate? Is she sleepy? Does she need to play? The following list gives you some other ideas for controlling mouthing and nipping:

➤ Whenever your puppy licks you, say "Kisses" and praise her warmly.

➤ Hold your attention when your puppy nips softly. Keep your hand still. Don't forget, hand withdrawal is an invitation to play and nip harder.

➤ If your puppy starts biting down hard, turn on her quickly, say "Ep, Ep!" and glare into her eyes for two seconds. Go back to your normal routine.

➤ Remember, puppies nip when they feel needy (just like a baby cries). If your puppy won't let up, ask yourself if she wants something, like an outing, exercise, or a drink. If all checks out and your puppy won't quit, crate or isolate her with a favorite bone. Do not scold your puppy as you isolate her. Calmly place your puppy in her area.

Training Your Puppy Around Kids

Kids act a lot like puppies. They're always on the floor and into everything. If you have children, teach your puppy not to mouth them from the start. Here's how.

Leave your puppy on a one-foot-long nylon leash whenever she's with your children. If she starts playing too rough, pick up the leash, snap back, and say "Ep, Ep." If you're still having trouble, buy a squirt gun or plant mister and fill it with water and vinegar. Spray your dog discreetly when she starts getting riled up.

If all else fails, give the puppy a time-out attached to you, stationed, or crated. Help the kids see that their restlessness leads to puppy withdrawal.

Older Puppies

Do you have a Peter-Pan pup, one who still nips past her time? Well, the buck stops here. After 14 weeks, there's no excuse. If your puppy's still nipping and you're the one who taught her, it's you who'll have to mend your ways:

➤ Stop all challenge games, including wrestling, tug-of-war, chasing your dog around, and teasing. These games teach dogs to clamp down hard on any object and challenge. This could be a leash, the laundry, your shirt, or even your skin.

➤ Correct all nipping, whether it's a bite on your arm or a nibble on your finger. Teeth do not belong on human skin, period.

➤ Put the Teaching Lead® applications in Chapter 8 into action. It's time for you to step up as the leader!

➤ Purchase a few weapons to use in defense, such as Binaca®, Bitter Apple® spray, or a long-distance squirt gun.

➤ Give yourself something to grab. If your dog's not wearing the Teaching Lead®, place a short lead onto her buckle collar.

➤ If your dog begins to mouth, turn to her, use a lead or collar to snap her head from your body, and say "Ep, Ep!" Glare at her for a second and then go back to business as usual.

➤ If she continues to nip, ask yourself: Do I look convincing? Am I snapping or pulling? (Pulling encourages play.) Is my dog taking me seriously? You may need more training before you earn her respect.

➤ Carry Binaca®. Spritz your dog whenever she's mouthing and say "Ep, Ep!" Spray her nose once or twice. After that, you can spray the air above her head; the sound will warn her off.

Curing the Chase and Nip

There are two categories to cover here:

➤ *The bathrobe assault.* If your dog's a clothing grabber, dilute some Bitter Apple® spray in a plant mister and carry it with you when you suspect your dog will pull this assault. Do not turn and face your dog when she jumps; this is interpreted as a challenge. Without looking or responding, spray your dog and continue walking. If this problem persists, get help now. It can develop into post-puberty aggression. No joke.

➤ *The child chaser.* Kids running around the yard, apartment, or house are a big temptation. If you were a dog, you'd be jumping and nipping too. Because you can't teach kids to stop being kids, you need to help your dog control her impulses. Put your dog on the Teaching Lead® and ask the kids to race around in front of you. Any time your dog looks tempted to lunge, snap back and say "Shhh." Repeat as often as necessary to gain control.

Still Having Trouble with Your Nipper?

If you're still having problems keeping your dog from mouthing and nipping, go through this checklist to ensure you're doing everything by the book. If nothing else works, get professional training help.

✓ Do not yank your hand away from your dog's mouth.

✓ Avoid physical corrections. They often encourage dominant play and lead to more aggressive reactions.

✓ Permit young puppies to mouth softly. Correct hard bites by emitting a startling vocal sound and either snapping their head from your hand or spritzing their mouth with Binaca® or diluted Bitter Apple®.

✓ Do not allow mouthing after 14 weeks.

✓ Kids aren't for mouthing. Period. Let your dog drag a leash when they play together and correct all rough play.

Two Feet, the Joyous Jumper

Everybody knows a jumper—a knock-you-over-when-you-come-in jumper, a muddy-paws-on-the-couch jumper, a counter cruiser (a dog who likes to sniff along counter tops). Jumping is a sure-fire attention-getter. So what gives? The first step in solving your problem is to understand how it became a problem in the first place. Once again, your dog's not to blame. Let's hop into his paws and see what's going on.

Remember, dogs see us as other dogs. Eye contact is a big method for canine communication. Our eyes are up high, so to be gracious and greet us properly, dogs must jump. The first time this happens, often in puppyhood, a hug follows. "Isn't that cute?" After about the tenth jump, it's not so cute. So the dog usually gets a shove. But what's a shove to a dog? Confrontational play. The dog jumps higher and harder the next time. So the human tries a little toe stepping, paw grabbing, yelling, all with the same effect; dogs think jumping is interactive and fun.

Counter jumping is another favorite pastime. After all, we're looking at the counter constantly, so why shouldn't the dog do so as well? When a dog jumps up, the human reacts by shouting and shoving. The dog interpretation? Prize envy. The dog thinks, "Whatever I was reaching for must be excellent because everybody raced over for it." So the dog reconsiders. He jumps when your back is turned or you're out of the room. Is this behavior spiteful? No, just plain smart. Now let's dissect and correct this problem one jumping situation at a time.

Your Homecoming

The best way to remedy jumping when you come home is to ignore your dog. Try it for a week. Come home and ignore your dog until she's given up. Keep a basket of balls or squeaky toys by the door. When you come in, toss one on the ground to refocus your dog's energy. If your dog's crated, don't let her out immediately; wait until she's calm.

If you have a big dog or a super-persistent jumper, put on an overcoat to protect yourself. Whether it takes two minutes or 20, go about your business until your dog calms down.

Do you have kids? Tell them to look for rain and do the same. Cross your arms in front of your chest and look to the sky. Don't look down until the coast is clear. Consistency is key. If one family member follows the program but the others encourage jumping, your dog will jump-test all visitors.

When Company Arrives

CHARLIE (the dog): "Oh boy! The doorbell. What fun! All eyes are on me. Paws flying everywhere! Oh no! Why are you putting me in the basement? What did I do? Bummer."

COMPANY: "Oh my gosh. This crazy dog. Why don't they train her? How unsettling."

It's a common routine. Nobody's in control. Nobody's comfortable.

First, be stern with your regimen and train your company how to act around your dog—and you thought training your dog was tough.

➤ *Practice doorbell set-ups.* Put your dog on her Teaching Lead®. Position someone at the door and ask him to ring the bell ten times at 20-second intervals. Tell the visitor to come through another door when he's done. Each time the bell rings, call your dog's name and walk away from the door. If your dog is a real maniac, try the chin lead (as described in Chapter 7) and discreetly spray her nose with Binaca Breath Spray® as you say "Shhh." Practice these set-ups twice a day until your dog tones down her reaction.

➤ *Create a greeting station.* Designate an area by the door to send your dog when company arrives. Secure a leash to the area and place a favorite ball or toy there. When the bell rings, station/secure your dog as you instruct "Go to your place" and answer the door. Instruct your visitors to ignore the dog while greeting you. Wait until your dog has calmed down to introduce her, even if it takes an hour.

➤ *Designate a greeting toy.* If your dog's a real tennis ball fanatic (or any other toy), withhold it until you have company arriving. Each time you enter your home or company arrives, say "Get your toy" as you toss it on the floor. Spritz your dog if she jumps and continue to ignore her until she's settled down.

Calming Attention Jumpers

If you can ignore your dog, the silent treatment is your most effective response. If I kept bugging you for a game of Parcheesi and you didn't look up once, I'd go elsewhere for fun. Once your dog lets up, encourage her by saying "Get your toy!" and let her pay attention to that. If your dog's a real nudge, keep a lead (short or long) attached to her collar. When she jumps, grasp the lead and snap your dog sideways quickly (this is called a *fly flick*) as you continue to ignore her. Give no eye contact, body language, or verbal corrections.

Discouraging Counter Cruisers

Do you have one of these? Counter cruising is a bad habit that's hard to break. Corrections actually encourage sneaky behavior. Though I've heard it a thousand times, your dog's not grabbing out of spite. The reason your dog grabs when your back is turned or you leave the room is so that she can avoid a challenge. Let me elaborate: Your dog sees your eyes and mouth (remember, hands = mouth) interacting with objects on the counters all day. When she copies you, you shout (again, remember, shouting translates into barking) and challenge her for whatever the prize is. Canine message? Whatever is on the counter must be great, but I better grab it when all backs are turned or they're out of the room or I'll have to give it up. Let's try to solve this problem with dignity:

1. With your dog on the Teaching Lead®, place something tempting on the counter.

2. The instant your dog looks up to sniff the counter, snap the lead back, say "Ep, Ep," and shout at the counter, "Bad turkey!"

3. Continue to work in the kitchen, correcting your
   dog whenever she even thinks about approaching
   what's on the counter.

Sarah Says

If mealtimes are too distracting to your
dog, station your dog while you cook.

If your dog's already on the counter, you're too late to correct her; instead, flick her off by curling a finger under her
collar or grabbing her lead. Don't yell at your dog once
she's on the counter. Don't lurch, shove, snatch, or hit.
Touching reinforces behavior. After all, a touch is attention.
If you push your dog, you'll reinforce her behavior.

Furniture Fanatics

Most people invite puppies on the furniture only to regret
it later. If you have a puppy and you don't want him on
your furniture permanently, do yourself a favor and discourage it from the start. If you have a delinquent furniture lover, the problem's not too hard to break. You'll just
need to be consistent.

Place your dog on the Teaching Lead® and walk up to
your couch or bed. The second your dog prepares for the
jump, snap back and say "No!" Encourage him to "Sit"
and pet him. Walk back and forth until he sits automatically. Try the same set-up with a family member on the
couch. Next, lead your dog up and sit down yourself. If he
goes to jump, snap sideways and ignore him until he sits
quietly. Reward his cooperation with a chew toy.

Still Having Trouble with Your Jumper?

If you're still having problems with a jumper, go through
this checklist to ensure you're doing everything by the book.

✓ Correct jumping before the jump! Nip it in the excitement phase.

✓ Control yourself! If you want your dog to stay calm, you must set the example.

✓ Train visitors to ignore your dog until she's calm.

✓ Use your Teaching Lead® to lead and station your dog around temptations.

The Bothersome Barker

A barking dog's a real headache and a complete nightmare. How you handle the situation will depend on what's prompting it in the first place. In the meantime, you need to watch your reaction. The cardinal sin when rehabilitating your barker is for you to yell. When you yell, your dog thinks you're barking, which leads to—you guessed it—more barking. A bark-along. To solve your problem, stay cool.

At the Door

Almost everyone appreciates a dog-alarm at the door and a few woofs to announce new arrivals. It gets annoying, however, when the alarm can't be shut off. The optimal situation would be to have an alarm bark with an off switch. Here's how:

1. Place a penny can or spray bottle (filled with a 50/50 mix of vinegar and water) at the door.

Doglish

OOOH...

To make a penny can, fill an empty soda can with ten pennies and tape the top. The shaking sound startles many dogs.

2. Position someone outside the door and ask him to ring the bell ten times in 20-second intervals.

3. When your dog starts barking, approach the door calmly. Spray her nose or shake the penny can discreetly as you say "Shhh!" and instruct "Back" to clear the greeting area. Approach the door calmly.

4. Keep your dog behind you as you open the door. Never hold your dog while you open the door. It will make her more wild.

5. Repeat as often as necessary to condition respect.

6. Now try it with the real McCoy!

If your dog is aggressive, please consult a professional. Aggression is a serious problem.

The Territorial Terror

Do you have one of these? Does your dog bark at everything he sees and hears? Start training immediately. Your dog needs to understand that you're the boss. Avoid leaving your dog alone outdoors for long stretches of time. Unsupervised confinement often breeds boredom and territorial behavior. Put those two together and you're likely to end up with a barkaholic. Block off areas that your dog uses as lookout posts, such as a living room couch or windowsill. If she's a night watchman, secure her on-lead in your room at night. Give her three feet of freedom—just enough to lie comfortably on her bed.

Screaming at your dog will be translated into barking. Your dog will feel supported and her role as leader (she barked first) will be reinforced. Any time you see (or hear) your dog start to perk up, say "Shhh" and call her to your side. If she ignores you, place her on the Teaching Lead® or let her drag a leash so you can quickly gain control. Use a spray mister or penny can to reinforce your verbal "Shhh!"

Car Problems

Being locked in a car with a barking dog is my version of purgatory. The car creates a fishbowl effect, similar to the territorial situation just described. Your dog barks and the passing object disappears, only faster in the case of a moving car! Yelling at your dog isn't the thing to do. Pleading won't win you any brownie points. This problem tends to disappear slowly as you progress through training, although there are a few things you can do in the interim to discourage this behavior:

➤ Have your dog pause before you let her enter or exit the car. Instruct "Wait" and give her permission to enter with "OK." It's your car, not hers!

➤ Enforce stillness while you drive. Station your dog in the car.

➤ Is your situation unbearable? Secure your dog on a chin lead (as described in Chapter 7).

➤ Ignore the barking if your car's moving. Driving is a job in itself.

➤ If you're stationary, spritz your dog with a spray mister or shake a penny can and say "Shhh."

➤ If your dog barks at gas-station or toll-booth attendants, ask them to toss a piece of cheese into the car window from afar. Hopefully, your dog will make a more positive association.

Attention or Protest Barking

Some dogs don't like to be left alone. This is especially true with adolescent dogs, but is also the case when older dogs have been pampered every time they barked. If you soothe a protest barker or dog that's barking for attention, you'll end up with a real spoiled brat on your hands. If you ignore the situation, your partner may threaten to leave you. Is there a happy medium? Well, not really, but I'll give it my best shot:

➤ Ignore it if you can. Never yell.

➤ Avoid grandiose departures and arrivals. They're too exciting.

➤ Dogs like to be with you. Avoid problems in your home by using the Teaching Lead®.

➤ Place peanut butter in a hollow bone and give it to your dog as you leave.

➤ Use a water pistol or toss a penny can toward (not at) your dog when she starts up. Be careful though, she can't know where it's coming from.

➤ Return to your dog only after she's calmed down. If you must interfere with her barking tantrum, go to her quietly without eye contact or comments, place her on the Teaching Lead®, and ignore her for half an hour while you lead her around.

Still Having Trouble with Your Barker?

If you're still having problems, go through this checklist to ensure you're doing everything by the book.

✓ Never yell at a barking dog.

✓ Make sure you place your feet in front of your dog's paws before a correction.

✓ Don't focus on your dog or make prolonged eye contact when giving a correction—eye contact reinforces behavior.

✓ Once your dog quiets down, respond by refocusing his attention or praising.

Chapter 11

Other Socially Unacceptable Behaviors

In This Chapter

➤ Digging, garbage grabbing, and gross eating habits

➤ Separation anxiety

➤ Stimulated sprinkling and timidity

Ingesting socks, digging to China—there is a common thread. Dogs do these things when they're anxious. Some dogs have anxiety due to lack of structure and some are more on the obsessive-compulsive side of life. Read this chapter, identify these problems, and do your best to help.

Digging

Digging can be a favorite pastime when your dog gets bored. It can also be a cry for company. Dogs don't like being left alone. They fuss, and fussy dogs dig. Unfortunately, you cannot teach your dog not to dig. Instead, you must give him a place that's all his own. Here are some suggestions:

➤ Pick one area where your dog can dig to his heart's content.

➤ Go to the area ahead of time and hide some favorite biscuits/toys.

➤ Go to the area with your dog each day, instructing "Go dig!"

➤ Have a dig-fest. Dig with your dog and cheer him on.

➤ If you catch your dog digging somewhere he shouldn't be, correct him with "No!" then tell him (escorting him to the right spot, if necessary), "Go dig!"

Spraying your dog with a hose or setting mouse traps is cruel and I don't encourage it. Putting the dirt back into the hole is confusing—now you're digging in the same spot too. Place your dog indoors when you garden. It's just too tempting after seeing you dig in one area all day!

Garbage Grabbing

Garbage grabbing is the perfect eye-catcher. It's very rewarding, and very annoying. To solve this problem, keep a lid on it. Keep your garbage locked away under the cabinets. Prevention is the best solution. No table treats before or after your meal. I know, the eyes are pleading and it'll go to waste, but if your dog can have it in his bowl, he'll want it in the trash.

If your dog is still rummaging around, try practicing one of the following set-ups:

➤ *Ten-foot line.* Place your dog on a ten-foot-long line and toss something irresistible into the trash. The second he starts to show interest, step on the line and shout "No!" Rush up to the garbage can and kick and scream at it. Do not yell or look at your dog. Go back to whatever you were pretending to do and repeat the process from the top. If your dog ignores the temptation, give him a hug.

➤ *Sound off.* If your dog is sound-sensitive, construct a pyramid of penny cans. Place ten pennies each in six cans and arrange the cans with three on the bottom, two in the middle, and one on top. Tie a string to the middle can on the bottom row and either attach it to the can or hold it. When your dog shows interest, pull the string and shout "No!" at the can.

➤ *Balloon pop.* The last thing to try is the balloon stay-away. Blow up a few balloons and pop them one at a time with a pin with your dog present. As each one pops, act afraid yourself. Don't pay any attention to your dog. Just act it out and trust me, he'll be watching. Next, tape the balloons to the edge of the garbage can and leave them there a couple of weeks.

Is your dog an angel when you're in the room, but crafty when you leave? Smart dog. Your timing is probably off. Are you correcting after he's stolen something? He considers your correction as prize envy and figures he'll take it when you're not around to challenge him for it. There are a few approaches you can try:

➤ Set up a bitter-tasting lure by soaking a paper towel in Tabasco sauce. Repeat this until he loses interest in the trash.

➤ Set up the penny-can pyramid and booby-trap him after you've left the room.

Inedible Ingestion (Pica)

Chewing sticks, rocks, and slippers is perfectly normal.
Eating them, however, isn't. If your dog is into swallowing
everything in sight or has a hard time passing up the kids'
underwear or socks, you are dealing with an obsessive-
compulsive behavior.

Sarah Says

If you own a dog with this problem, you'll
have to keep a close eye on him. If you
think your dog has eaten something non-
digestible, call your veterinarian immediately. These items can block the intestine
and, if left untreated, kill your dog.

I call it *prize envy*. When your dog grabs something he
shouldn't, you think, "Bad dog, give it back!" Your dog,
however, sees your body language from a dog's perspec-
tive. He thinks you're racing forward to steal what he's
found. If he wants to keep it, he better split or gulp it.
Some split. Others gulp it, whatever "it" is. To stop this
behavior permanently, you may need to seek professional
help. Until then, follow these guidelines:

➤ Do not chase after your dog angrily for anything.

➤ Place favorite treats in small party cups and distrib-
ute them around the house.

➤ If your dog picks up something he shouldn't, grab a
party cup and encourage him to come to you and
exchange the object for a treat.

➤ If you notice something tempting on the ground,
don't dive for it. Remember, you're setting the example. Try to distract your dog and remove it calmly.

Separation Anxiety

Separation. Dogs hate it. If they had their way, they'd follow you to the ends of the earth. But alas, they can't. Dogs suffering from this condition may chew destructively, soil the house, bark excessively, or act out other destructive behaviors. It's not spite. Dogs can't think that way. It's anxiety, canine style. If you're experiencing this problem, your dog will fall into one of two categories:

➤ *The passive dog.* This dog clings to his owners when they are home, often soliciting attention and getting it. He interprets this love on demand for a desire to be led. This leads to over-identification, not unlike a child who clings to his mother's leg. This dog is confused about himself and depends on people to reassure him. When they go, so does his identity.

➤ *The dominant dog.* This fellow thinks he is king of his castle, ruler of the roost. When his owners, whom he considers his subordinates, leave, his anxiety is in their best interest. "How will they survive without their great leader there to protect them?"

This problem must be resolved with training. Training will give the passive dog a sense of identity and the reassurance that a competent leader is on the job. Training will place the dominant dog in a subordinate, carefree pack position. If you need help training, get it. In the meantime, follow these ground rules:

➤ Never correct your dog after the fact. Never. Corrections are not connected to the destruction; they're connected to your arrival. This makes your dog more anxious the next time you leave.

➤ Avoid theatrical hellos and good-byes. Lavishing your dog with kisses, biscuits, and drawn-out declarations of devotion do not reassure him. They stress him out.

➤ Leave a radio playing classical music to cover unfamiliar sounds.

➤ Place your dog in a dimly lit area to encourage sleep.

➤ Leave a favorite chew toy. Rub it between your palms for scent.

If you're leaving for over six hours, try to find someone to walk your dog. Otherwise, proof the house from her destruction; buy an indoor pen. They fold nicely to store when you're home and can be expanded before you leave to give your dog space when you're gone for extended periods. Dogs get cramped if left in small kennels for longer than six hours and can develop Hyper Isolation Anxiety.

When home, temporarily decrease the attention you give your dog by 50 percent. Do not give in to solicitations. Although it relieves your feelings of guilt, it is too sharp a contrast from leaving your dog alone all day.

Next, you'll need to set up practice departures. Station your dog in a familiar spot. Instruct "Wait" and leave the room for 15 seconds. Return and ignore him until he's calm, and then praise him lovingly. Repeat this ten times or until he stays calm.

Continue these short separations until he shows no anxiety. Double the separation time and repeat the procedure. Continue doubling the departure time until you're able to leave the room for 30 minutes.

Sarah Says

Once he's comfortable at 30 minutes, go back to short separations, but this time, leave the house. Gradually work your way up to 30 minutes out of the house. Start over, this time getting into and starting your car. With patience, you'll be able to build his confidence and leave him for longer and longer periods of time.

Stimulated Sprinkling

Do you have a tinkler? The most frequent question I've been asked is, "Do they grow out of it?" Well, yes and no. Yes, if you handle yourself properly, and no if you don't. Tinkling isn't a conscious thing. Dogs do it because they are overexcited or anxious. Discipline your dog for doing it and you'll make it worse.

When you come in, ignore your dog until she's completely calm. Extend a jar of peanut butter or a cup of biscuits as you pet her. Divert her mind. Kneel down to pet her rather than leaning over.

If your dog is timid around certain people, have everyone (including yourself) ignore her. When you soothe her, it reinforces the fear. When your dog approaches the person, offer her treats. Use a shake cup or peanut butter jar. When she is calm, have guests kneel and pet her chest.

If your dog piddles during greetings or play sessions, ignore her or stop the play until she has better bladder control.

Timidity

Timid dogs look so pitiful. Like kids, you want to soothe them. But dogs are not kids; they'll think your soothing is a sign of your fear. Now you're both afraid. That's a big problem.

To help your dog, you must act confident when she is afraid. You're the leader. Stand up straight. Relax your shoulders. Breathe deep. Smile. Whether it's a bag blowing in the wind, a sharp noise (like thunder), or an uncommon face, act calm, face the feared object, and ignore your dog until she starts to act more like you.

If your dog is showing aggression when she's fearful, call a professional. Do not knowingly put her in threatening situations.

Thunder

There are ways to handle thunder phobias. Let me start with the don'ts. Don't coddle your dog. Don't permit him to hide between the sheets or climb onto the couch. Don't isolate him. These make the fear worse. Depending on how bad your situation is, try one or all of these approaches:

➤ Turn on some classical music and play it loud.

➤ Lead your dog on his Teaching Lead® while you act completely calm. Set the example. Show him how to cope with the situation. Let your dog have his fears, just don't respond to them. When he calms down, pet him lovingly.

➤ Find (or make) a thunderstorm tape recording. Play it on low volume while you play your dog's favorite game with him. Slowly increase the volume.

➤ Ask your veterinarian for tranquilizers to soothe your dog before a storm.

Chapter 12

Where to Go for Help

In This Chapter

➤ Seeking advice from your veterinarian, groomer, or pet store

➤ Finding a class to fit your needs

➤ How to recognize a good trainer

Finding the right help for training, if you need it, is essential. Training is a joint effort for you and your dog. My clients would be the first to tell you that it's a blend of the right actions—from how you hold the leash to your tone of voice to the way you stand—that helps your dog learn what you are trying to teach. When I'm training people to work with their dogs, I harp on the little things until they are doing them instinctively. If my harping doesn't come through in the pages of this book clearly enough, get help—the right help, as described in this chapter.

Amateur Trainers

It's funny, actually. As soon as people know you have a dog, they become experts. Promise me one thing: No matter what they say, no matter how convincing, regardless of how many parlor tricks their dogs know, don't listen.

Grrr

Free advice never pays. If you try a little of this and a little of that, guess who's going to suffer? You'll make your poor dog crazy.

Ask for training advice from a vet, groomer, or pet-store owner, and you may get an off-the-cuff, routine answer, but nothing that is tailored for your individual situation or dog. Instead of asking these other professionals for training tips and solutions, ask where you might find a reputable trainer or classes in your area.

Sniffing Out a Good Dog Trainer

Finding a good trainer—one who is well-rounded in his or her knowledge of dog behavior—can be a real lifesaver. If you need help training your dog, scout out professionals in your area to get some good leads and call today. You and your dog will be glad you did! The following sections look at a few of the training options that are available to you.

Personal Trainers

I'm a personal dog trainer. I train more than dogs, though; I train people. When looking for a personal trainer, you're looking for someone to train you (as well as your dog). These are some of my training ethics, which I recommend looking for in any personal trainer:

➤ Put yourself in your client's shoes.

➤ Know that the client is trying to do the right thing.

➤ Understand the dog's personality and listen to what the dog is trying to say with his behavior.

➤ Know when you can't help. Be honest with your client.

➤ Help your client understand why the dog is behaving inappropriately. Help the client think for his dog.

➤ Teach the client Doglish so he can communicate with his dog.

➤ Help the client structure his home.

➤ Teach the client patience, tolerance, understanding, and sympathy. After all, he loves his dog.

Not all trainers are in this profession because they love dogs first and foremost. Some are in it primarily for the money. Beware.

Grrr

If you seek help, make sure you avoid trainers who encourage discipline.

Group Training

Group training class can be a real blast. It can also be a dog owner's worst nightmare. So what's the deciding factor? The instructor. When exploring different classes, talk to the instructor and get a feel for his or her style of training. Here are some questions you can ask:

➤ How many dogs are in the class?

➤ Are the classes divided by age?

➤ Do you have a favorite breed of dog or do you have experience with a wide variety of breeds? This can indicate a strong bias on the part of the instructor.

➤ What do you teach in class?

➤ Are the classes indoors or outside?

➤ Do you have different class levels?

➤ Are behavior problems discussed?

Sarah Says

People often ask me what the best way to train is, group or private? Honestly, it's a combination of the two. A private consultation lets me see how things go on a day-to-day basis. Class gives me the opportunity to follow up on that session while the dog learns around distractions.

➤ Do you have a make-up policy?

➤ Is family participation encouraged? Can the kids come?

The class size should be limited and must be divided by age and experience. I offer Puppy Kindergarten classes for dogs under six months, Grade School for inexperienced pupils, and High School and College for advanced students. I limit my class size to eight. Make sure your instructor is not breed-biased. Your dog should be seen as a unique and special personality, not a stereotype. Your instructor should be versed in breed-specific tendencies, however, and help you understand your dog's individual character. He or she should also help you understand how your dog relates to your entire family and encourage them to participate in the training.

Books and Videos

Are you a do-it-yourself person? I'm all for it as long as you follow the right advice. Obviously, since you're reading this book, you have some faith in my methods, but not everyone suggests a positive approach to training. Be selective when choosing your reading material and call for some help if matters don't improve. You'll only train your dog once, so do it right!

Sarah Says

Videos are the wave of the future! They're easy to follow and can be watched by the whole family. There's even a companion video to this book (to order it, see the form in the back of this book).

Chapter 13

What Good Dogs Know

WAG WAG
WAG

In This Chapter

➤ Here at my Heel

➤ What "No" really means

➤ Don't move an inch: Sit and Stay

➤ Come (please)

➤ Hit the dirt: Down

Here are the basics. These are the bare-bone facts your dog must understand and you must learn how to teach him. I'll walk you through each command one step at a time. I suggest you practice each command five minutes a day. Your dog may pick up certain things quickly and take weeks to learn others. That's how it usually goes, so don't get frustrated. Think of what you're accomplishing. You're teaching another species your language. Be patient. Dogs learn best from an understanding teacher.

Heel

It's a beautiful thing to watch: a dog standing calmly at his owner's side, walking when he moves and sitting when he stops. Yes, it can happen for you too, if you're patient. Although it takes a while to synchronize, eventually you'll be maneuvering through crowded streets and calling your dog to heel at your side from a distance. Sound miraculous? It all starts with one small step. Use the exercises described next to train your dog to stay at Heel.

The Merry-Go-Round

Practice this heeling exercise in a non-distracting environment (it can be indoors or outside). Clear an area to walk in a circle. Position your dog in the starting position: sitting straight at your left side, toes aligned, your heels ahead of the dog's front paws. You're ready to begin!

1. Relax your arms, let them hang straight at your side, and keep your thumb behind your thigh. Use a snap correction the instant your dog wanders from the heel spot.

2. Command "[Name], Heel" as you begin to walk in a counterclockwise (dog on the inside) circle.

3. Walk in a forthright manner—head held high and shoulders back—to communicate leadership.

4. Praise your dog for watching you or snap the leash to encourage focus.

5. Stop after each circle by slowing your pace and reminding "Heel." Place your dog into a sitting position. (To position your dog when you stop, grasp the base of the leash—where it's attached to your dog's collar—with your right hand and use your left hand to position his hindquarters.)

6. Practice five circles twice a day.

Grrr

If your dog turns to face you when you stop, guess what? He's facing off. Another attempt for control. To discourage this habit, grab the base of the leash with your left hand. Step back on your left foot and swiftly swing your dog into the proper position. Now you can praise!

Change It Up

When you're preparing to stop, lift your left foot high in the air (like you're marching) and stamp it lightly on the floor. This will give your dog an added clue that he's suppose to stop and sit.

Move faster by trotting. Slow your pace by lengthening your stride. Make sure you change gears smoothly and indicate the change by saying "Easy." Remember your dog's a dog, not a Porsche!

At normal speed, command "Heel" and pivot to the right. To help your dog follow you, slow down as you turn and cluck, bend your knees, or slap your leg. Make it interesting! Avoid choking him through the turn—that's no fun! Walk on six paces and stop and hug your dog—good job!

Big-Time Heeling

You'll know you're ready to practice the Heel command in everyday situations when your dog responds without pressure on his collar. Then try it in new situations.

For example, keep a short lead on your dog around the house. Pick it up and command "Heel" as you're walking around. Have your dog finish in the proper sitting position. Then release him by saying "OK" and give him a big hug! Or, practice heeling for one-quarter of your morning walk. Keep your hand behind you. No sniffing or lunging at neighborhood pals. Finally, you can practice in a parking lot. Make sure it's not too crowded.

Do things get out of hand when you're in public? If so, calm down! If you yell "Heel, Heel, Heel" and jerk your poor dog back and forth, of course he'll get excited. Wouldn't you? Ask yourself, "Am I asking too much too soon? Does my dog need to exercise more before we practice in public? Is my left arm straight and behind my back?" If your left hand is in front of your thigh, your dog will be too. Then he's the leader, not you!

No

Many dogs think "No" is the second half of their name: "Buddy No! Tristan No! Molly No!" There are a few inconsistencies with the way people use this little word that leaves dogs baffled as to its meaning.

For starters, "No" is usually shouted. Shouting to a dog sounds like barking. Would barking excite a situation or calm it down? "No" is used with the dog's name. In my book, you should only use your dog's name when you're happy, not mad. "No" is said after the action has occurred. If I yelled at you after you ate a bowl of soup (or even while you were eating it), would you understand that I was upset at you for opening the can? "No" said at the wrong time communicates nothing. Finally, "No" is said repetitively; "No, No, No, No," sounds different than "No," again confusing dear doggy.

Sarah Says

If you don't like to say "No," use another word or sound. Just be consistent. Personally, I like "Ep, Ep." It sounds softer, but the dog gets the message "Don't even think about it!" loud and clear.

What's an owner to do to teach a dog not to get into trouble? Fortunately, I have the answer. To teach your dog this concept, you must set up situations to catch your dog in the thought process. First we'll work indoors; then we'll go out.

Indoors, put your dog on his Teaching Lead®. Have someone secretly place a piece of cheese on the floor in a neighboring room. This is your prop. Follow these steps and pay attention to timing!

1. Bring your dog into the heel position and casually walk toward the cheese.

2. The second your dog notices the cheese, snap back on the lead and say "No!"

3. Continue to walk like nothing has happened. Remember you're the boss. No means No.

4. Walk by the cheese several times to ensure that your dog got the message.

After your indoor training, practice "No" when you're out for a walk. When your dog notices a passing jogger, car, kid, another dog, or two tidbits (disguised as squirrels) climbing a tree, say "No" just like you did with the cheese. Sidestep away from the temptation to emphasize your snap. Continue to snap each time the antennas flicker. Praise your dog for focusing on you and relaxing his radar system.

Stay

Is this your dream command? You're not alone. I'm not sure why people have so much trouble teaching this one, but it's probably because it's rushed. They teach it one day and expect their dog to stay while they welcome company or walk into the kitchen for a sandwich. Promise this: You won't rush. Taught progressively, this one's a real winner. To prepare for your first lesson:

➤ Take your dog into a quiet room. No TV. No kids. No cats. Just the two of you.

➤ Slide your dog's neck collar high near your dog's head and center it between his ears.

➤ Fold the leash in your left hand to hip level.

➤ Position your dog behind your heels.

Now you're ready to teach your dog his first lesson! You'll do six commands. No more, no less. Here are a couple of rules for your dog's sake.

Look over your dog's head when you practice; never look directly into his eyes. It's too daunting. Stand tall. When you bend, it looks like you want to play. Stay close to your dog when you start out, about six inches from toe to paw. Creating too much distance too soon can be really scary. While doing each exercise, hold the lead directly above your dog's head. If he confuses "Stay" with "Go," you'll be ready for a quick correction. Vary the length of each pause. If you don't, your dog will think smart and break ahead of time. He's just trying to please! Resist petting your dog until you finish the following steps. Too much petting will ruin his concentration.

1. Command "Sit." Align your dog with your ankles.

2. Command "Stay" as you flash your hand in front of your dog's nose. Remove the signal and pause for five seconds. Command "OK" as you swing your arm forward and step out of position.

3. Again! Command "Sit, Stay." This time, pivot to face away from your dog and pause ten seconds. Return to the starting point, and release. "OK!"

Sit down and Stay put.

4. Back again. Command "Stay." Pivot in front of your dog. Pause. Now march. Yes, march, slowly at first, like you're sleepwalking. Once your dog holds still for that, start marching like a proud soldier.

5. Command "Stay" and pivot and pause. Now try jumping and waving your arms. Go slowly at first; ease into it.

6. Now for some noise. Pivot, pause, and then bark at your dog. Remember, no staring; keep looking over his head. Add a meow or two when he can handle it. Return, pause, and release!

7. From your starting position, command "Stay," pivot in front, and pause for 30 seconds. Stand up tall, relax your shoulders, and keep the leash above your dog's head just in case he's tempted to break. When the time is up, return to his side, pause, and release with "OK!" Now it's time to hug that dog.

Practice this simplified sequence twice a day until your dog's feeling mighty fine about his accomplishments.

Come

Now for everybody's most desired command. First you need to ask yourself a couple of things. Have you said "Come" more than once and yelled it repeatedly? Have you chased your dog and bribed him with his favorite delicacy? If so, trouble is brewing. Your dog thinks "Come" means disobedience; Come = Game Time! Fortunately, you can straighten him out, but it will take some time, concentration, structure, patience, and a lot of praise. If you think you have what it takes, read on!

Come Front

Like "Heel," "Come Front" is taught as a position near you. This time, your dog should be facing you and looking up. Whether you're calling your dog from two feet away or across the yard, he should come and sit down, paws facing toes, eye to eye. To teach your dog what "Come" is all about, start with a simple exercise that you'll use throughout the day. Practice it in the house to start.

1. Walk in front of your dog while he's standing calmly.

2. Standing tall, say "[Name], Come" as you tap your foot and zip your finger up your belly from his nose level to your eyes. Make a funny sound to encourage focus.

3. If he comes but doesn't sit, guide him into the proper position by lifting up on his buckle collar and tucking his hindquarters into position.

4. Once your dog sits and makes eye contact, give him a big hug!

Repeat this exercise throughout the day, whenever you have something positive to share—a pat, treat, dinner, or toy. Make sure your dog's first associations to this word are warm and welcoming.

Grrr

If you must position your dog, lift his collar gently and squeeze his waist muscles below his ribs as you press down. Avoid jerky motions and pressing his backbone. Do not command as you position.

Distance Control

No, you're not off-lead yet. Be patient. Prerequisite? Your dog must understand that "Come" means a specific spot in front of you, looking up. Mission accomplished? Practice this exercise in a quiet room. No TV. No kids. No cats. Keep your lesson short and upbeat:

1. Practice three regular "Sit-Stays." Return to your dog's side and release him with an "OK!"

2. Leave your dog in a "Stay" and walk out to the end of the leash.

3. Pause. Vary the duration each time.

4. Call "[Name], Come!" in a directional tone. Signal it by sweeping your right arm across your body.

5. As soon as you've issued the command, scurry backward and reel in the leash.

6. When he gets near your feet, signal up your belly and tap your heel to the floor (as described earlier) to encourage a "Sit" finish.

7. Encourage eye contact by standing tall and making kissing sounds.

8. Release him with "OK." Good dog!

Practice "Come" three times per session. That's all. More
is stressful. Remember to blend each "Come" call with a
few regular "Sit-Stays." If you don't, your dog will break
his "Stay" early to please you. Sweet thing.

Troubleshooting the Come Command

Here are a few things to remember when teaching this
command:

➤ *Use it sparingly.* When it's overused, dogs stop paying
attention.

➤ *Don't chase your dog if she doesn't respond!* Practice
on-lead for now.

➤ *Never call for negatives.* Do you have to brush, bathe,
or isolate your dog? Don't use "Come." Avoid using
it if you're angry. You'll only freak her out.

➤ *If your dog runs away, don't repeatedly call or correct
her!* I know the frustration of marching around in
the middle of a cold, wet, rainy night looking for
your dog, but if you call or discipline your dog,
you'll only be teaching her to run from you.

➤ *Use a different command to bring your dog inside.* Coming in from outdoors is a big drag, paralleled with
being left alone or ignored. Using the command
"Come" would make it a negative. Instead, pick a
command like "Inside." Start using it on-lead when
bringing your dog into the house. Quickly offer a
treat or ball toss.

Distraction Come

Does your dog get excited when she hears "Come"? Good
job. Now you can start encouraging focus around low-
level distractions and increasing the distance from which
you call her. Here are some ideas (see if you can add to the
list): Try it in front of the TV, in the backyard, in front of
the kids, and during mealtime. In a quiet hallway/garage,

attach the Flexi-Leash® or a substitute, and increase your distance slowly.

Using the "Come" command around distractions is a taller order than your living room version. Most dogs try to pay attention to the distraction and you at the same time, which is impossible. If your dog's torn, say "No" and snap the lead when your dog turns toward the distraction. Praise him when he focuses on you: "Good dog!"

Though "Come" is the command of the hour, don't forget to sandwich each exercise between a couple of normal "Sit-Stays." If you call your dog from each "Sit-Stay," he'll anticipate your request and since you can't correct a dog that's coming at you, you're stuck. Prevent the problem by working a few "Sit-Stays" between each "Come" command.

Are you having trouble getting your dog's attention around distractions? You're not alone. It's a hard nut to crack. My advice: Stick with it. Don't give up. You must communicate that there's only one way to "Come" and that is to sit directly in front of you. Practice in a quiet room for a day, enthusiastically praising your dog's focus. Next, try it with your TV on:

1. Leave him: "Stay."

2. Pause at least a minute (building up anticipation).

3. With a straight back, deep voice, and gigantic hand signal, call "[Name], Come!"

4. Flag him in. If he sits straight, praise him happily!

5. If not, sidestep from the distraction, snap the chain firmly, and say "No."

6. Encourage and praise any focus immediately.

Work up the distraction chain slowly. If your dog's too stimulated, practice around simpler distractions for a while. There's no rush. It's not a race. And whatever you do, don't get frustrated! Frustration kills enthusiasm.

"Come" is a funny thing. If used too much, dogs resist it. When your dog understands the command, avoid using it all the time. Say it infrequently and make it extremely re-warding! (Don't forget your other commands too: "Inside" for coming indoors, "Let's go" for follow me, and "Heel" for staying at your side.)

Down

Whoa, Nellie! That's what the "Down" command says. Once you can get your dog to do this, you're really on your way. "Down" is also a sign of respect. Sound dreamy? It's easier said than taught, however, because the issue of trust also comes into play. For a dog to lower himself into a submissive, vulnerable position, he must be really sure you're the competent leader you say you are. Will you stand up to the scrutiny? We'll see...

Your dog's first "Down" lesson will be simple. You expect nothing; you're just showing your dog what the word means. You say it and help him into position over and over until he gets the picture. There are different strokes for different folks; pick the procedure that suits you best. Once you decide, practice two or three times a day, four "Downs" per session.

Sarah Says

Training a young dog makes it easier. Young, passive dogs are the easiest to persuade. Brutes, young and old, are more difficult. Am I giving you nightmares already? Good. Now that you're prepared for the worst, you may be in for a pleasant surprise.

The Easy Slide. This one is great for easy-going dogs or pups.

1. Instruct "Sit" and kneel down at your dog's right side.

2. Draw a quick line from your dog's nose to the floor and say "Down."

3. Place your left thumb between his shoulder blades and gently lift a paw forward with your right hand as you firmly press between the shoulder blades. Your dog should slide himself to the floor.

4. Don't pet your dog yet! Pause five seconds, verbally praising him quietly.

5. Release with "OK," stand up, and hug your dog. Good dog!

Teaching an easy-going dog to lie down.

The Side Swipe. If your dog locks up on the Slide, try this method:

1. "Sit" your dog and kneel at his right side.

2. Draw a quick line from your dog's nose to the floor and command "Down."

3. Reach your left arm over your dog's back and place each hand on a corresponding paw.

4. Lay your left forearm across his shoulder blades.

5. Gently lift your dog's paws as you apply pressure with your forearm.

6. Re-command "Down" as you're positioning.

7. Pause five seconds, while praising verbally.

8. Release with "OK," stand up, and praise.

Look, No Hands! Does your dog think he's Jaws? If so, try this option:

1. Sit your dog and stand perpendicular to his right side.

2. Drop the leash-slack on the floor and calmly slide it under your left foot. Fold the remaining slack in your left hand.

3. Command "Down" as you point to the floor.

4. Pull up on the lead continually, forcing your dog's head down.

5. Most give in at this point. If yours does, praise verbally, pause, and release with "OK!"

6. If your dog doesn't respond, press his shoulder blades until he collapses into position. Hold the slack under your foot for five seconds. Release and praise.

Sarah Says

Once your dog begins cooperating, use "Down" for everything: before treating (hold the treat to the ground and command "Down"), dinner (cover the bowl with your hand and, as you put it down, say "Down"), or a Toy Toss (hide it in your hand, hold it to the ground, and command "Down").

The Upright Down

At this point, your dog should go down whenever you give the command—if company is visiting or when you're eating dinner, out in the yard, or at the veterinarian. Remember, "Down" communicates two things: "Calm down" and "I'm the leader." Now that he's had time to learn the word, you can give this command from a normal upright position:

1. Sit your dog, pivot perpendicular to him, and casually slide the lead under your left foot (gathering the slack in your left hand).

2. Stand straight and point to the ground as you command "Down" sternly. DON'T BEND! Pull the lead under your foot continually.

3. Praise for cooperation, pause, and release with "OK." (If your dog refuses, press down on his shoulder blades.)

4. Now it's time to change your position! Pivot six inches in front of your dog.

5. Slide the lead under your foot.

6. Lift your arm above your head. Point swiftly to the ground as you command "Down." Pull the lead gently if necessary. Press his shoulders if he refuses.

7. Pause, praise, and release.

Once your dog's responding well at six inches, pivot out one foot and repeat these steps. Then pivot two feet, four feet, six feet, and so on. You're on your way!

Once you can instruct your dog "Down" at three feet, you're ready to start using the command in some everyday situations. Here are some ideas (add to this list): before you sit down to pet your dog, at night while you're watching TV or reading, or when your dog comes over for his goodnight kiss.

Sarah Says

Remember the ratio: One command = one action. If your dog responds, praise him lovingly. If he doesn't, position him calmly. Avoid getting frustrated; it only adds fear to an already stressful situation.

Now we're talking! Start using the "Down" command to settle your dog whenever he gets restless or a situation feels too out of control. Here are some things that flash to my mind (add to the list): when company's visiting, at the veterinarian, when there's a sudden change in the environment, outdoors, and when he gets overstimulated. Start with small distractions, such as squirrels, and work your way to big ones, such as other dogs, the mail carrier, and joggers!

Advanced Moves

No one can underestimate the pleasures of a well-trained dog. Master the basics in Chapter 13 before you begin the exercises described in this chapter. As you work toward off-lead control, don't get too bold. You'll have less control. Your dog has a choice. If he doesn't want to come and he's free to run, you may be standing there helpless. Off-lead work means constantly reading your dog and being aware that your dog is reading you. To have control, you must look like a leader; be confident and self-assured, so your dog will want to trust your judgment.

To further your mental preparation, keep these three steps in mind:

➤ *Stay cool.* Frustration makes you look weak. As you wean your dog to off-lead commands, your dog may act confused and unresponsive. There is a reason. You used to give the command and guide her with the lead. Now, something's missing. It will feel awkward. Whatever her reaction, stay cool. Any corrections will add to her confusion. Jazz up your body language and use some pep talks to encourage her toward you.

➤ *Stay focused.* Eye contact communicates control. Your dog should be watching you. If the reverse is true, you're the follower. To avoid this, make sure you're working in a confined area so that you can ignore your dog when she disobeys. A graceful retreat is not a failure.

➤ *Step back.* Your dog is responding off-lead beautifully until...someone rings the bell, a chipmunk runs across the drive, or another dog's around; then everything's out the window. You're back to being ignored. Let me tell you a secret: Off-lead control takes time. If your dog is good, but still having trouble in a stimulating situation, use your Teaching Lead®. Using it helps control the situation while simultaneously conditioning more appropriate behavior.

Using Some New Equipment

As you work toward off-leash obedience, you'll be practicing exercises that extend your control to farther and farther distances. Before you start, round up these items:

➤ *Flexi-Leash®.* This retractable leash is invaluable for advanced work. The longer, the better.

➤ *Tree line.* You attach this 20-foot line to a tree and practice distance command control. Purchase a canvas leash or make your own out of a clothesline attached to a dog clip, which you can purchase at a hardware store.

➤ *Long line.* You'll be using this 30-foot line for distance control with "Wait," "Heel," "Down," and "Come" commands. Purchase a canvas lead or use a clothesline.

➤ *The short lead.* This is an additional training tool. It should be long enough to grab, but short enough to not distract your dog.

Grrr

Attach all lines to your dog's buckle collar, not to her training (choke) collar.

Off-lead dogs aren't created overnight. Training is a step-by-step process. You'll be using your new equipment to increase your dog's focus, but don't get itchy fingers. Just because she behaves well on her Flexi-Leash® one day doesn't mean she's ready for an off-lead romp the next. Take your time. Although I'll explain how to train with each piece of equipment separately, you should use them interchangeably in your training exercises.

Training with the Flexi-Leash®

This leash is a great exercising tool. It allows freedom to explore, while still leaving you in complete control. As a training tool, you can use it informally during walks to reinforce the following commands:

"[Name]." Call out your dog's name enthusiastically: "Daisy!" If she looks at you, praise her. That's all that's required. Just a glance. If she ignores you, snap the leash, say "No," and then praise her once you have her attention.

"Wait." Begin to command your dog to stop 3 feet in front of you with this command. If your dog continues forward, snap the leash and say, "No, wait." Increase your distance to 6 feet, 8 feet, 12 feet, 16 feet, and 26 feet in front of you.

"Sit-Stay." Use the Flexi-Leash® to increase your distance control. Increase your distance incrementally.

"Heel." Use this command to call your dog back to your side. Call out her name and then command "Heel" as you slap your leg. Praise your dog as she responds, then walk a short distance before you stop to release her.

"No." Whenever your dog's focusing on something she shouldn't be, snap the leash and say "No!" Immediately refocus her attention with a toy, stick, or command.

Training with the 10-Foot Line

Use this line while you're keeping an eye on your dog. Every couple of minutes, stand by the line and give a command ("Sit," "Down," "Wait," or "Come"). If she looks confused, step on the line, and praise her anyway as you help her into position. For example, if you command "Down" and she gives you a blank stare, praise her as you guide her into position. Your understanding will help her overcome her off-lead confusion.

If your dog gives you some defiant canine backtalk (a bark or dodge), step on the lead, snap it firmly as you say "No," and station and ignore her for 15 minutes. She's been grounded with no TV!

Control with the 10-foot line.

Practice Indoors with the Short Lead

Use the short lead indoors after your dog's reliable on the 10-foot line. When it's attached to your dog's buckle collar, you can use it to reinforce your stationary commands: Sit, Stay, Down, Wait, Heel, and Come.

In addition to using the short lead around the house, do a lesson once a day. Bring your dog into a quiet room and practice a command routine. Initially, hold the short lead, but then drop it once you've warmed up. Slap your leg and use hand signals and peppy body language to encourage your dog's focus.

Branching Out with a 20-Foot Tree Line

Tie this line to a tree or post. Secure all knots. Leave the line on the ground and follow the sequence described next.

Warm up with five minutes of regular on-lead practice. Stop your dog next to the tree line and attach it to your dog's buckle collar discreetly. Remove her regular lead and place it on the ground in front of her. Keep your hands free.

Command "Stay" and walk ten feet away. Extend your distance as she gains control. Run your fingers through your hair and swing your arms gently back and forth to emphasize that your dog is off-lead. As your dog improves, practice an out-of-sight "Sit-Stay." Practice "Down" from a "Sit-Stay" and a "Down-Stay." The command "Come" can also be practiced, but never call at a distance greater than the line will reach.

If she falls for this and darts for a quick getaway, wait until she's about to hit the end of the line to shout "No!" Return her back into position and repeat the exercise at a closer range.

If your dog disobeys, determine whether her response is motivated by anxiety, confusion, or defiance. If she's confused or anxious, do not issue a correction. Calmly return to her side and reposition gently. Repeat the same exercise at close range. If your dog breaks defiantly, however, either shout "No" as she hits the end of the line or, if she's baiting you, return quietly and snap the lead as you say "No." Reposition and repeat the exercise at close range for quicker control. Good luck!

The Big 30-Foot Long Line

Now for some outdoor stuff. Attach your dog to the 30-foot long line and let her roam free as you keep a watchful eye. Engage her by playing with a stick or ball and investigate your surroundings together. Avoid over-commanding. Just hang out and enjoy some free time with your dog. Every five minutes, position yourself near the line and issue a command enthusiastically.

Sarah Says

Practice in an enclosed area. It only takes one mistake to lose your dog; until she's an off-lead expert, she may get confused.

If it's a stationary command, like "Sit," "Wait," or "Down," stop abruptly and stamp your foot while giving the command and signaling. If it's a motion command, like "Come" or "Heel," run backward as you encourage your dog toward you. If she races over, help her into the proper position and give her a big hug. If your dog ignores your command, quickly step on the line and say "No." Don't scream; just speak sternly. After your correction, give your dog the opportunity to right her reaction before lifting the line to snap it or reel her in. End your session with a favorite game.

Those Nagging Questions About Off-Lead Training

Before I address questions, let me warn you: Practice all initial training in an enclosed area. When you start off-leash, your dog may turn into a little comedian and bound away from you just for fun, so keep it safe until he's reliable. You may be wondering many things at this point. Here are a list of questions I'm asked most often:

> **When will I know that I can trust my dog off-lead?** You should feel it. It's never a smooth road in the beginning; some days you'll get a quick and happy response, others will feel more like your first day of training. Stay cool, though. Frustration is a sign of weakness and you'll lose your dog's respect. Keep your dog enclosed as you practice so that if she starts to act cocky, you can retreat immediately. And

don't hesitate to go back to Long Line or Teaching Lead® exercises for quick review.

Can I use treats for the off-lead stuff? I don't recommend it. Treats become very addictive and, as you'd soon find out, dogs taught with food are less responsive when the food's not around. Training should focus your dog on you, so make yourself the treat!

There are times when my dog crouches and barks at me. Don't look at her. She's trying to turn all your hard work into a game. Ignore her until her antics subside. Work her on the Teaching Lead® if she's being impossible.

Don't the lines get caught around trees and doors? Yes they do. Clip all lines to the buckle collar and never leave your dog unsupervised.

When I go to position my dog, she stays just out of reach. Watch that body language and negative eye contact. Being off the Teaching Lead® is nerve-wracking for both of you. Look at the ground as you return to your dog. If she's still out of reach, kneel down and wait. When she approaches, take her collar gently, reposition, and work at close range.

My dog picks the end of the line up in her mouth and prances around me like a show horse. Clever girl. Try soaking the end of the line in Bitter Apple® liquid or Tabasco sauce overnight. If she's still acting cocky, quietly go inside and watch her discreetly from the window.

Emergency Down

This exercise can be a real lifesaver once your dog learns that when you say "Down," you want him to drop as though he's been shot. In the beginning, it can be a little confusing; so be patient and positive throughout your training process. Don't start practicing this exercise until your dog has mastered the Down command.

1. Stand next to your unsuspecting dog.

2. Suddenly command "Down" in a life-threatening tone (the type of tone you'd use if a loved one were about to walk off a cliff). Point toward the ground.

3. Kneel down quickly as you bring your dog into position.

4. Act like you're being bombed too!

Grrr

This exercise is very stressful! Limit your practice to one out-of-the-blue Emergency Down sequence a day.

Soon your dog will catch on and act independently. Once she does, begin extending your distance from her. Eventually, this exercise could save your dog's life if you were ever separated by a road and her life was threatened by an oncoming vehicle. It's true! The Emergency Down really does save lives. Once I was leaving my training classes with my husky, Kyia, when a tennis ball slipped loose and started rolling toward the road. Kyia, sweet thing, wanted to help and ran innocently to collect it. In a panic, I shouted "Down" and she dropped like she'd been shot. What a good girl!

Chapter 15

Beyond the Backyard

In This Chapter

➤ Going public

➤ Car manners

➤ Greeting dogs and people

➤ Scary things

Training's biggest reward is the freedom it gives you to take your dog everywhere! Your dog will be a welcomed social guest, a plus at parades and picnics, and an added fan at after-school sporting events.

Dogs don't transfer their lessons from the living room to public appearances. They need to be taught how to behave in social situations. In this chapter, I'll cover this type of training.

Going Public

Before you jump right in, you'll need to prepare yourself. The first trip out can be a real embarrassment. You'll feel self-conscious, your dog will be too distracted to listen, and you'll feel compelled to tell everyone, even those who aren't paying any attention, that your dog's in training. How do I know? I've been there.

Before you hit the streets, you should practice in selective areas so that you can devote all of your attention to your dog. Eventually, it will seem effortless and your dog will truly be welcomed everywhere. But your first trip out may be a real shocker. Are you wondering, "If it's such a nightmare, why bother?" There are three reasons:

➤ It gets easier.

➤ A well-mannered dog is fun to share.

➤ It enhances your dog's focus. You'll be the one looking confident in new, unexplored territories.

The first outing with your perfect-at-home pal may feel more like his first day of training, but don't be discouraged. Think of it as a test to determine if those house rules apply everywhere. Even I had the "first-outing blues" with my dog Calvin. As I was trying to steady his Heel, I walked straight into a light post. Ouch!

I'm going to draw you a map that guides you from putting your dog into the car to the ride home. I'll walk you through step by step. But before we begin, there are some universal rules to keep in mind:

➤ Keep your dog on his Teaching Lead®. His leash reminds him of good behavior. No fancy stuff or showing off, please. There are too many dangers!

➤ Use lots of encouragement. Cheerfulness is contagious.

➤ Paws behind heels! Remember, you lead and he follows.

➤ Keep the communication flowing. Commands provide structure.

➤ No elimination in public. Take care of that activity at home. Bring a bag just in case of accidents!

➤ Know when to say "No" to both your dog and other people.

I know it sounds like a lot. Once you get the hang of it, though, it'll seem like second nature. It's all about leadership.

Car Manners

The first step in shaping your perfect public partner is getting him to the destination with your sanity intact. If some of you are chuckling, it's no wonder. Most dogs are less than cooperative in the car. Jumping from seat to seat and barking at passing strangers is the norm.

Put yourself in your dog's paws. To him, your automobile is a window box with wheels. And while passing cars, pausing for bicycles, and braking for squirrels is part of your normal routine, it pushes his chasing and territorial instincts to the max! Whether he barks or bounces, the predator whizzes away. Conclusion? He's victorious—the champ! Not only do they run away, but they run fast! You haven't even gotten out of the car and your dog's already pumped. See where the problem starts?

Where does it end? Negative corrections don't work. Yelling is perceived as barking. Besides, discipline and driving don't mix. To solve this problem or to train a fresh dog or pup to behave, follow this routine:

1. Lead your dog to the car with the command "Heel."

2. Open the door and command "Wait." Pause.

3. Say "Go to your spot" and direct your dog to a car station.

4. Secure your dog on a car lead and tell him "Stay."

Now you can proceed. Things always go more smoothly when they're organized. Now it's time to get out of the car. Again, from your dog's paws, the situation is pretty exciting—new sights, smells, and faces. Don't take it personally if he doesn't notice you or listen to commands at first. Getting him focused is the challenge at hand:

1. Before you open the door, instruct "Wait."

2. If he jumps forward, catch the car lead, say "No," and snap it back.

3. Re-instruct "Wait" and pause until he's calm.

4. Put on his Teaching Lead® and say "OK" as you let him exit.

Sarah Says

Attach the clip to the buckle collar or chin lead. Do not clip the car lead to a training collar.

5. Immediately instruct "Heel," bringing him to your side.

6. Instruct "Wait" as you shut the door.

7. Proceed with "Heel." Now you're walking in style!

Car Fear?

Cars really frighten some dogs. It's a worrisome problem. The cause usually goes back to being transported at an early age, but it can result later in life too. If your dog suffers from this, avoid pacifying or being overly forceful. Both reinforce fear. If you must take him somewhere, pick him up if possible or take him to the car while he's napping. Speak or sing softly. Have the car already pulled out with classical music playing on the radio. Equip his area with a familiar blanket and a favorite toy.

Refusal?

Does your dog refuse to hop into the car? Well it's understandable if your dog's a tiny tot, but if you have a 120-pound Great Dane, you're being taken for a ride. You have to make a stand not to lift him ever again. If you do, you're forcing him into a state of learned helplessness. Lead him to the car, taking some of his favorite treats along, and try baiting him in. If this makes little impression, get in the car and, as you bribe him, pull him gently forward. Still no luck? Bring a friend along, pass the lead to her through the car, and have her gently pull as you encourage him forward. If he still resists, physically walk each limb into the automobile one at a time, but under no circumstances lift!

Once You Get There

Once you get to your destination, the first five minutes is three-quarters of the battle. Whatever practice location you've picked—a park, town, friend's house, or building—first impressions really count. If you take control immediately and give understandable directions, the rest will be a tail wag.

Grrr
Your dog must be vaccinated before taking him out. Many deadly diseases are airborne and vaccinations are your dog's only protection against them.

Let's pick up where we left off. You've just brought your dog into a Heel after shutting the car door. Instantly, your dog will probably have one of two reactions: he'll become wild or he'll become a scaredy cat.

The Wild One

If your dog is the wild type, his nose will be twitching a mile a minute, he'll pivot toward every new stimulation, and pull to investigate every blade of grass. Here's a way to control your Huck Finn:

➤ Enforce "Heel." Keep his paws behind your ankles at all points.

➤ Tell strangers to back off until your dog's trained. It's embarrassing, I know, but it's a must. You don't want Buddy jumping up and giving someone a scratch, even by accident.

➤ Reinforce your requests. If you ask for a "Sit-Stay," get a Sit-Stay.

Take all commands back to the introductory stage, no matter how well you're doing at home. Initially practice only "Heel" and "Stay" commands.

Scaredy Cat

If you have a passive or scared dog, the experience of arriving at a new place may seem overwhelming. His tail may disappear, his body may lower, and, when stimulated, he'll try to hide behind you. If you bend to soothe your scaredy cat, you'll be reinforcing his reaction. It's so tempting to soothe him, I know. Just keep saying to yourself over and over, soothing reinforces fear, soothing reinforces fear. Instead:

1. Look confident and stand tall like a good leader dog. Soon he'll mimic you!

2. Bring some treats and a favorite toy along to focus his attention on. Withholding them at home makes the new adventure seem really exciting!

3. Use "Heel" and "Stay" commands often; familiar sounds soothe anxiety.

4. If he's too nervous to listen, enforce a response without corrections.

5. Stay calm and positive. Deflect any admirers until he's feeling safe.

Troubleshooting Your Arrival

Having some trouble? Here are some questions I often get:

Heel! Are you joking? He does it great at home, but he's a maniac everywhere else! There are two remedies for an out-of-control Heel:

➤ *The side-step.* Whenever your dog is focusing on something to your left, take a giant step to the right, snap the lead, and remind "Heel." The bigger or older the dog, the sharper the snap. Repeat until your dog's alert to you. Praise that!

➤ *The kick back.* If you have a charging brute on your hands, lock your left hand to the back of your thigh. The second he moves forward, remind "Heel" as you thrust your left leg back. Don't kick him, though; just move your leg in the opposite direction as you remind "Heel." Repeat until he stays behind your leg.

If you're still having problems, consider a different collar or try holding the lead behind your back.

Greeting People

Stop shaking. This doesn't have to be a hair-raising experience. Before I talk you through this, though, please read over the following disclosures. If you identify with any of them, please follow my specific instructions and skip the rest of this section.

First disclosure. If you're having aggression problems, the only person you must introduce your dog to is a trainer with a specialty in aggression rehabilitation. How do you find such an expert? Ask your veterinarian. It's better to be safe than sued.

Second disclosure. If you notice your dog getting nervous or tense around unfamiliar people, join a class or work under private supervision. Don't push the issue alone.

Third disclosure. If you don't believe it will work, it won't. Hire some extra help to build your own confidence!

If you're still with me, here are five key rules to follow when that dog of yours makes his debut:

➤ *Rule #1.* Make sure your dog is familiar and comfortable with the setting before attempting to introduce him to anyone. Don't greet people your first day out!

➤ *Rule #2.* Feet ahead of paws! Correct all attempts to scoot forward.

➤ *Rule #3.* Tell admirers what you're doing: "We're in training."

➤ *Rule #4.* Stay more focused on your dog than the admirer. Correct all attempts to break.

➤ *Rule #5.* Put faith in your own knowledge. Just because everyone has advice, that doesn't mean it's right. "I don't mind if he jumps" doesn't hold water. You mind! Period.

Now for the actual greeting. How you handle the situation will depend on none other than your dog. If your dog is overly enthusiastic, you'll need to tame his expressiveness. Keeping him focused on you is the key.

Greeting a Wild One

Ask people to wait until your wild one is calm. Enforce a "Sit-Stay," keeping your feet ahead of his paws. Place your left hand, fingers down, along his waist and below the ribs. Using your right thumb to brace his collar, hold him steady in case he jumps. If the person still wants to, he can pet your dog! Remind your dog to "Stay" and don't let up your vigil until the person is gone. Whew—what a workout!

Greeting a Scaredy Cat

Ask your greeter to wait until you and your dog are in position. Place your dog in a "Sit-Stay" and kneel down at his side. Put your left hand on his waist and your right hand on his chest, holding his head up for confidence as the greeter pets him.

Help with Greeting Problems

If your dog is a little cautious when people approach, before you start, place some treats in your pocket. Ask the person to wait until you and your dog are positioned. Enforce a "Sit-Stay," keeping your feet ahead of his paws. Once he's steady, ask the person to give him a fist full of treats without attempting to pet him. If he seems comfortable, pet him together as you hold his head upright with your left hand. If he still seems nervous, quit while you're ahead! You'll get there.

Sarah Says

If your dog's nervous, bring along some goodies or, if he likes peanut butter, bring along a jar. Have your greeter give him some to win his approval.

As he gets more confident, wean him off his treat dependency. Use one with every other person, then every third person, and so on.

Encountering Other Dogs

Are you shaking again? Envisioning your dog hurling himself at the end of the lead? Well, wake up! You're having a nightmare.

If you've had some stressful encounters in the past, try to put them behind you. Memories cloud control. Wipe the slate clean. If you see a dog when you're out and about, don't approach it immediately. First, get control of your situation:

1. If your dog acts excited, snap the lead firmly and remind "Heel."

2. Continue in your original direction and pick up your pace.

3. Don't look toward, approach, or follow the other dog.

4. If your dog continues acting wild, speed up and keep snapping.

5. Praise him for focusing on you.

6. Never give in or let up!

Letting Your Dog Greet Other Dogs

Once you have your dog under control, you can permit a greeting by saying, "OK, go play!" Before you do, though, make certain the other dog is friendly and the other owner is respectful of your training efforts. When playtime is over, instruct your dog to "Heel" and move on.

If your friend has dogs and you want to get the dogs together to play, let them meet each other on neutral ground, such as an empty playground or field. This prevents a fierce territorial reaction. When they first meet, you should expect a lot of bluffs, such as growling, mouthiness, and mounting. Don't choke up on the leads. It's natural. Interference might prompt a fight. Stay calm, but observe closely. The dogs must determine a hierarchy. Once that's accomplished, they'll settle down. If you're certain a fight has begun, separate them with the leashes. Don't handle fighting dogs.

If You're Approached

If you're not in the mood or your dog's too hyped, just say no. If you're game, however, get your dog in control behind you and then release with an "OK, go play!" Call him back to "Heel" when playtime is over.

If You're Approached by an Off-Lead Dog

If you're approached by an off-lead dog, don't hesitate, don't look at the dog, and don't let your dog look at the dog. Just walk quickly away from the area. Discourage any confrontational attempts your dog makes by snapping the leash and walking faster. Both of you should avoid eye contact. An off-lead dog defends his territory. If you leave without confrontation, he'll stop the chase immediately to harbor his fighting reserves for a more threatening foe.

Entering Buildings

Pick a building you might visit with your dog: the veterinarian's office, hardware store, pet supply store, or your kids' school. Your dog's behavior in those buildings will depend on who enters the building first. Yup, that's it. If your dog leads you, then he's in charge. If you lead your dog, then you're the head honcho. Whoever *starts* in charge *stays* in charge.

Sarah Says

Some dogs are nervous when they enter new buildings. If your dog's showing fear, show confidence. Don't pet him or reassure him things will be okay. Instead, take along some treats to encourage him as you approach the building. Stand tall and ignore his caution. If he puts on the brakes, kneel down and encourage him inside.

1. Bring your dog to a "Heel" as you exit the car.

2. As you get to the threshold, brace your arm behind your back. (Dogs sense when they're going somewhere new!)

3. Say "Sshh" if he starts getting excited.

4. Pause before you open the door and command "Wait."

5. Don't open the door until he's settled down.

6. Re-command "Wait" as you open the door.

7. If your dog lunges, snap him back sternly and say "No!"

8. Pause again until your dog is calm.

9. Say "OK" as you lead him through.

Curb Etiquette

Whether you live in a city or not, eventually you'll run across a curb. Applying our usual psychology, some restraint is in order here!

1. As you approach the curb, your dog should be in a "Heel."

2. At the curb, instruct "Wait."

3. If your dog continues, snap the lead and say "No, Wait," pulling him behind your ankles.

4. Say "OK" as you lead him across.

5. Remind "Heel."

To keep your dog behind you, hold the leash behind your thigh.

Common Fears

One of the cutest miracles I get to perform is teaching pups to handle stairs. I'll tell you my secret. Once your puppy is large enough to handle stairs, avoid carrying him. Instead, brace his rib cage securely in your hands and help him to manipulate his body to do the action. Don't forget to praise him while you do. If yours is really frightened by the whole flight, carry him to the bottom few steps and ask someone to kneel below to coach him forward.

Some dogs fear people in uniform. To help him overcome his fear, act very friendly toward uniformed people. Ask them to help you socialize your puppy as you give them some treats to offer to him. If they're willing, ask them to kneel and avoid eye contact until he's sniffed them out. Another great trick is to rent a uniform from a costume shop and dress up in one yourself!

Some dogs fear people of a particular sex. This problem results from any number of circumstances. Generally, they all fall under either inappropriate or lack of socialization with a particular sex. If this happens at home, place your dog on his Teaching Lead® during arrivals and follow the directions given for uniformed people. If the problem doesn't improve or if you notice any aggression, seek professional help.

Whatever the cause, make sure that you use your dog's favorite treats for the introduction. Try this approach (we'll use a man for the example):

➤ Instruct the man to avoid direct eye contact with your dog.

➤ Do not force the situation. Act cheerful and cordial to the man, setting a good example.

➤ Casually place a treat on the man's foot and praise your dog if he takes it, or ask the man to hold out a jar of peanut butter and let the dog approach. No staring allowed!

➤ Eventually, when your dog initiates the interaction, try petting him together.

If your dog is afraid of children and the problem doesn't improve with the following suggestions, find a private trainer who has experience with this problem. Practice your "Heel" and "Sit-Stay" commands around the perimeter of a playground. Do not let the children approach.

Grrr

If your dog tenses up, his eyes grow cold, or he starts to growl, do not work him around children until you are under the supervision of a professional trainer. Don't become another statistic. Dogs that bite children are often euthanized.

Act like a child with your dog. For example, poke him or pull his ear like a child would do, squeal in a high-pitched voice, and stare at him at his level by kneeling or crawling. Once he's socialized to these patterns, he'll be more accepting when the children do it. If your dog's nervous around babies, borrow a friend's baby blanket (for the aroma) and wrap a doll in it to carry around the house, including your dog in all the fuss!

Condition your dog to the sound of his treat cup. Allow kids to take the cup and toss treats to your dog. If he's enthusiastic, let the children toss treats toward him. You can let him take treats gently from the children.

Impressing Your Veterinarian

I'll let you in on a secret. Veterinarians love a well-behaved dog. It makes their job a lot easier. To impress yours:

1. Bring your dog's favorite chew in case you have to wait.

2. When you get to the office, your dog will probably be excited or afraid. Instruct him to "Heel" at the car and enforce a "Wait" at the entrance.

3. Say "OK" and remind "Heel" as you check in.

4. If you must wait, place him in a "Town Down" under your legs and give him his favorite chew.

5. Instruct "Wait" as you go into the examination room to keep him calm and focused!

Some dogs aren't wild about receptionists and aren't too impressed by the DVM. Set up a practice run and ask the receptionist to meet you outside. Give her your dog's treat cup and ask her to avoid making eye contact with your dog. If your dog is tense, avoid confrontation. If your dog wants to approach, have the receptionist reward him with treats.

Going for an Overnight Visit

Taking your dog with you on an overnight visit can be a lot of fun or it can be a disaster. It all depends on how you handle the situation. Do some predeparture planning; pack a bed, a crate, chew toys, treats, leads, and a small portable radio. Yes, a radio; it drowns out any unfamiliar sounds and soothes his anxiety while you're gone.

When you arrive, greet everyone calmly or leave your dog in the car with the radio playing. Enforce a "Sit" for greetings and a "Wait" at all thresholds. When you go to your room, set up the crate or sleeping station. Offer your dog his treats and toys. Set up the radio next to his area.

If possible, avoid crating immediately. After setting up the bedroom, lead him around the outside perimeters and play a familiar game. If you must go, place your dog in his area with a chew toy and turn on the radio. Make sure you depart and arrive calmly. No overly theatrical guilt-trip scenes, please.

Doglish Glossary

About Face   A 180-degree turn to face the opposite direction. This is one of the moves practiced while heeling.

American Kennel Club (AKC)   A club that registers pure breeds and licenses dog shows, Obedience trials, and other competitive events.

Anchoring   A position you put your dog in to calm him down.

Bitter Apple®   A bitter-tasting spray that can be used to deter dogs from chewing on things such as leashes and furniture.

Body Language   Dogs have different postures for different modes—play, tension, and relaxation. Knowing how to interpret each will allow you to become a better teacher.

Buckle Collar   Adjustable collar made of cotton, nylon, or leather for your dog's tags. They do not slide or choke.

Car Station   A special area in the car for your dog. You should secure him here for his own safety and your own peace of mind.

Chin Lead (a.k.a. Halti, Promise Collar, or Gentle Leader)   A collar that helps control rowdy, mouthing dogs in the most humane and natural way.

Come Front   The first step in teaching the command "Come." The dog is seated facing his owner and looking up.

Delighted Tone   A praising tone to soothe your dog and make him feel proud.

Directive Tone   A tone in which you command your dog, clearly and directly, while standing in the peacock position.

Discipline Tone   A disapproving tone used with a constant expression, such as "Ep-Ep."

Down   This command requires a dog to lie down.

Electric Fence   An invisible barrier around your yard; an underground wire that creates a shock in the dog's collar when he approaches the edge.

Emergency Down   This command is a fast "Down" and is used in case of an emergency.

Excuse Me   A command to use if your dog crosses in front of or behind you, presses against you, or blocks your path. It communicates hierarchy.

Eye Contact   Eye contact is a key part of your dog's language, Doglish. The main principle behind eye contact is that you reinforce whatever you look at.

Flexi-Leash®   A retractable lead (16–26 ft.) that allows extended freedom *with* control.

Four Paw Rule   The technique of training a dog not to jump when greeted. This is accomplished by not petting your dog until *all four paws* are planted on the floor.

Frustrated Territorial Aggression   When a dog is put in isolation and cannot give his normal greeting response, he becomes even more assertive than he normally would be.

Group Training   Training your dog with a group of other dogs in an obedience class.

Habituation   The process in which a behavior becomes a habit because the dog is rewarded with attention (negative or positive).

Heel   In Heel position, a dog is aligned with the owner's left side; the dog's paws should always be behind his owner's ankles.

Hierarchy   A system of submission and dominance that dogs establish among one another. This is pack behavior that stems from their ancestors, the wolves.

Housebreaking The process of training a dog to eliminate outside or on paper.

Hyper Isolation Anxiety (HIA) Dogs who are over-isolated suffer from lack of stimulation and direction. This creates anxiety, canine style, which results in hyper behaviors, such as destructive chewing, excessive elimination, barking, or digging.

Kick Back A step back taken by the owner to force the dog into a good heel position.

Leading A technique used with the Teaching Lead® to establish control and dominance over your dog.

Let's Go A command used whenever you start walking (casually, not heel) or changing direction.

Long Lines Long leashes for gradual off-leash training.

Negative Attention The principle that even if you give your dog negative attention, such as "No!" for an unwanted behavior, it is still attention and the dog will learn to repeat this behavior.

No Pull Harness A harness that tightens around your dog's underarms when he pulls. It is an effective way to curb pulling on leash, although it's not an effective training tool.

Nylon Training Collar An "original" training collar made of nylon; these collars work best on fine-haired dogs with sensitive necks.

Original Training Collar (a.k.a. the "Choke Chain") A chain-linked collar that tightens around your dog's neck when pulled. It is the sound of the collar, not the restraint, that teaches.

Peacock Position The position from which to give your dog commands; stand tall like a peacock with your shoulders back.

Penny Can An empty can filled with ten pennies that's used to startle a dog when he's doing something inappropriate.

Prize Envy Confrontation, canine style. If your dog is holding something and you approach threateningly, he assumes that whatever he has in his mouth must be valuable because you are challenging him for the prize.

"Self-Correcting" Collar (a.k.a. the "Prong Collar") This collar is for dogs who are insensitive to pain. It is ideal for dogs who continually choke themselves on the original training collar.

Settle Down This command is used when instructing your dog to calm down at your side or go to his designated station.

Shelter Shock The traumatizing effect of being in a shelter can leave some dogs low-spirited and problematic.

Short Lead A short (8-inch) lead that can double as a car lead. It is a great way to control your dog around the house when he's running free.

Sit A command used to make your dog sit.

Stationing A special area in each room that is your dog's designated space. He is told to "Settle down" and secured with the Teaching Lead® or another leash.

Stay The command that requires a dog to stay in the same position for a certain amount of time.

Stimulated Sprinkling A subconscious release of urine; stimulated when excited or afraid.

Teaching Lead® A leather leash patented by the author. It is specially designed to attach around your waist or to a stationary object. It helps keep your dog with you when you're home so you can train him passively.

Tone There are three types of tones that your dog understands: delighted, directive, and discipline.

Treat Cup A cup with treats in it. This method is an effective way to get your dog to give you what he is chewing or biting on.

Wait and OK A command used to control your dog in doorways, on curbs, or on stairs.

Zipper Snap The sound of the original training collar (choke chain) when used correctly. It is this sound that teaches the dog, not the restraint.

Choosing a Breed: A Questionnaire

Your name: _____

Number of adults in family: _____

Number and ages of children (under age 18): _____

Your daily schedule (hours at home):

_____

Your leisure activities:

_____

_____

_____

Will you include the dog in these activities?

❏ Yes ❏ No

I have other pets.

❏ Yes   ❏ No

If yes, what kind?

_____ Age _____

_____ Age _____

I've owned a dog before.

❏ Yes   ❏ No

I've had success training a dog.

❏ Yes   ❏ No

I live in a(n)

❏ Large house ❏ Small house ❏ Apartment

I have

❏ A large yard ❏ A small yard ❏ No yard

Please enter one of the three following responses to the activities listed below.

Very little   **Moderate amounts of**   **Extensive**

I have time for a dog that needs _____ grooming.

I have time for a dog that needs _____ training.

I have time for a dog that needs _____ attention.

I have time for a dog that needs _____ exercise.

Please check the appropriate response:

I'm getting a dog to be

❏ A family member   ❏ A watchdog
❏ Used for work (type of work: _____)

I'd like a dog who is _____ of children.

❏ Very accepting   ❏ Tolerant, but aloof

I'd like a dog who needs _____ affection.

❏ Very little   ❏ Moderate amounts of   ❏ Much

I'd like a dog who _____.

❏ Is naturally active   ❏ Enjoys quiet walks
❏ Doesn't need extensive exercise

I'd like a dog who is _____.

❏ Eager to please   ❏ Independent   ❏ Strong willed

I'd like a dog who is _____ with guests.

❏ Enthusiastic   ❏ Calm   ❏ Reserved
❏ On guard   ❏ Indifferent

I'd like a dog who is _____ strangers.

❏ Naturally protective around   ❏ Accepting of   ❏ Aloof toward

When we go on trips, the dog would be _____.

❏ Taken along   ❏ Kenneled   ❏ Left with friends or family

I'd prefer a dog who sheds _____.

❏ Very little   ❏ A couple of times per year
❏ Shedding doesn't matter

I'd like a dog whose coat is _____.

❏ Long   ❏ Short   ❏ Thick   ❏ Feathery
❏ Curly   ❏ Wiry   ❏ Any of the above

Index

D-E-F